ADVANCE PRAISE FOR
IMPEACHING THE PRESIDENT

"Hirsch's lucid prose and careful analysis make the book a fine corrective to cavalier popular rhetoric surrounding discussions of impeachment."

—*Publishers Weekly*

"*Impeaching the President* is lucid, balanced, and deeply informed. Anyone in search of a reasoned guide to the unreason of our current situation should read it."

—Elizabeth Kolbert, Pulitzer Prize–winning author of *The Sixth Extinction: An Unnatural History*

"In an era when the notion of impeachment is tossed around as the ultimate political indictment, Alan Hirsch guides us with a steady hand through our own history to consider the three presidents who faced that ultimate punishment. This is a sober, precise, and carefully argued analysis that should be read by every member of Congress—and every president."

—David K. Shipler, former reporter for the *New York Times* and Pulitzer Prize recipient

"Alan Hirsch brings clarity, wisdom, and wit to a contentious and critical subject. *Impeaching the President* is must reading for all concerned citizens."

—Howard Shapiro, former FBI General Counsel

"Incredibly readable, well-researched, analytically sound and important."

—Alan B. Morrison, Associate Dean for Public Interest & Public Service at the George Washington Law School

Impeaching the President

Past, Present, and Future

Alan Hirsch

Open Media Series | City Lights Books

The Open Media Series is edited by Greg Ruggiero.

Special thanks to John Richard and Essential Information.

Cover image: One of the earliest known photographs of the White House, by John Plumbe, Jr., 1846.

Library of Congress Cataloging-in-Publication Data
Names: Hirsch, Alan, 1959- author.
Title: Impeaching the president : past, present, and future / Alan Hirsch.
Description: San Francisco : City Lights Books, [2018] | Includes
  bibliographical references.
Identifiers: LCCN 2018026391 (print) | LCCN 2018035420 (ebook) |
ISBN 9780872867635 | ISBN 9780872867628
Subjects: LCSH: Impeachments—United States. |
Impeachments—United
  States—History. | Presidents—United States. | Johnson, Andrew,
  1808-1875—Impeachment. | Nixon, Richard M. (Richard Milhous),
  1913-1994—Impeachment. | Clinton, Bill, 1946—Impeachment. |
Trump, Donald, 1946—Impeachment.
Classification: LCC KF5075 (ebook) | LCC KF5075 .H57 2018 (print) |
DDC 342.73/068—dc23
LC record available at https://lccn.loc.gov/2018026391

City Lights Books are published at the City Lights Bookstore
261 Columbus Avenue, San Francisco, CA 94133
www.citylights.com

CONTENTS

INTRODUCTION

The idea of impeaching the 45th president surfaced during the 2016 presidential election before we even knew who that president was going to be. Opponents of Hillary Clinton made no bones about their desire to push impeachment should she win, based on her use of a private e-mail server when she was secretary of state. Similarly, opponents of Donald Trump maintained that his extensive personal business holdings disqualified him from faithfully serving in the public interest as mandated by the presidential oath of office. Calls for Trump's impeachment on this and other bases began almost before he had completed his inaugural address. His impeachment became a more realistic prospect a few months later with the appointment of special counsel to investigate possible criminal activities perpetrated by the Trump campaign.

Throughout 2017, as Special Counsel Robert Mueller indicted several high-ranking officials in the Trump campaign and transition, commentators warned that the nation was headed for constitutional crisis. Debates broke out that went to the heart of U.S. democracy. What would happen if President Trump pardoned all those indicted?

Special Counsel for the U.S. Department of Justice Robert S. Mueller III.

What if Trump attempted to pardon *himself*? What if he fired the special counsel before the latter completed his investigation? What was to be made of the claim by President Trump's personal attorney, John Dowd, that "the president cannot obstruct justice because he is the chief law enforcement officer under [the Constitution]?"[1] Critics responded that Dowd's view puts the president "above the law" and thus contradicts a fundamental premise of the U.S. Constitution. Who was right?

Such questions, once fodder for law school exams and scholarly musings, have immediate relevance for our republic today. Fortunately, in addressing these questions, we do not write on a blank slate. The philosopher George Santayana famously observed that those who cannot remember the past are condemned to repeat it. The more optimistic version is that, by learning from history, we can shape a better future. We must, therefore, revisit the scope, purpose, and history of presidential impeachment.

This book looks in depth at the impeachment sagas surrounding Andrew Johnson in 1868, Richard Nixon in 1974, and Bill Clinton in 1998, in order to draw lessons for future impeachments. We then apply those lessons to the circumstances surrounding Donald Trump, mindful that we face a constantly evolving situation. First, though, we need to place impeachment within a broader context.

The genius of the U.S. constitutional design lies largely in the numerous interlocking clauses that protect against the tyranny that can result when any person or group obtains too much power. Such protection starts with the division of government into two separate spheres of authority, federal and state, and the division of the former into three separate branches with specific responsibilities.

But the founders knew that even this careful division of power would not establish sufficient protection. Congress only makes laws, but what if it passes laws that suspend elections or instruct the courts how to decide cases? The president has executive power only, but what if he uses such power to harass or intimidate the other branches? The courts only decide cases, but what if they wantonly strike down Congress's laws and the president's executive actions? Because limiting the authority of the three branches might not suffice, the founders also gave each branch means of keeping the others from overstepping.

The greatest risk of tyranny comes from the executive branch, in part because the president is a single person. Members of Congress and the Supreme Court cannot accomplish anything unless they persuade a majority of their colleagues to go along. In addition, the president's authority includes command over law enforcement and the military. For these reasons, maintaining restraints on presidential power is crucial.

Preventing tyranny preoccupied the nation's founders in part because of oppression by the British monarchy. King George III mistreated not only the colonists, but also his own people. One goal of the Constitutional Convention was to prevent monarchy by another name. In fact, some delegates opposed making one person responsible for executing the nation's laws. While the Convention eventually decided in favor of a one-person executive, it adopted a series of provisions designed to make the president a temporary public servant, account-able to the laws of the land.

Perhaps most significantly, the president would serve only a four-year term, requiring periodic approval of the voters if he or she wished to remain in office. But recognizing that great damage can be done in four years, the founders also provided a mechanism for quicker re-placement of the president if necessary. Specifically, the House of Representatives could "impeach" the president, an accusation of wrongdoing that would initiate a trial in the Senate. The Senate, in turn, could by two-thirds vote convict the president, which would automatically result in removal from office. (Congress can impeach and remove all federal officers, not just the president, but presidential impeachment was the framers' chief concern.)

Thus, the U.S. Constitution gives Congress the ulti-mate check on presidential power. At the Constitutional Convention, Virginia delegate George Mason captured the significance of this tool with a pair of rhetorical ques-tions: "Shall any man be above justice? Above all, shall that man be above it, who can commit the most exten-sive injustice?"[2] Alexander Hamilton directly tied the im-peachment remedy to the goal of avoiding monarchy: "By making the executive subject to impeachment, the term monarchy cannot apply."[3] A king, after all, could not be impeached.

We should not take the impeachment tool for grant-ed. While not unique to the United States, it is far from universal. When Richard Nixon resigned from office in

1974 under threat of imminent impeachment, many foreign leaders were bewildered. They assumed throughout the Watergate affair that, if he had to, Nixon could use his vast power to secure his position. In many countries, it is difficult if not impossible to remove a leader short of an insurrection or coup.

England invaded the United States and burned down the White House in 1814, but we have never experienced an insurrection or coup against a president. Instead, when the executive is believed to have abused power, we resort to impeachment—a pillar of our democracy and a peaceful means of protecting popular sovereignty. Even the president, this uniquely powerful and privileged person who commands the military and lives in luxury at the public expense, can be brought to heel. Nixon's downfall, while posing a national crisis, affirmed a transcendent principle. The People exiled from power a man who had won a 49-state electoral landslide less than two years earlier. The notion that no person is above the law, which in ordinary times sounds like a utopian ideal, suddenly seemed very real.

But like any potent tool, impeachment is dangerous if misused. It can be used to subvert the ballot box and to bludgeon a president disliked by Congress. Nixon's resignation was a victory not for a particular party or ideology, but rather for the American people and our institutions. In contrast, many historians view the two actual presidential impeachments, Andrew Johnson's in 1868 and Bill Clinton's in 1998, as partisan disasters in which the abuse of power came less from the impeached president than from his impeachers.

If impeachment can showcase the country at its best or worst, what separates the two? History offers guidance. In the pages ahead we revisit and draw lessons from the three major presidential impeachment episodes. We also address the other means of removing an unfit president: the 25th Amendment, which provides for temporarily removing a president who is "unable to discharge the powers and duties of his office." We begin, though, by seeking to learn from the founders.

FIRST PRINCIPLES

Most experts on the U.S. Constitution believe that a sitting president cannot be indicted and tried for a crime. Hauling presidents into court to face criminal charges would distract them from their responsibilities and undermine their authority as head of the executive branch. A one-person head of state must always be on duty, even when on a golf course seeking rest and rejuvenation. The president is at all times accompanied by a military officer carrying a device that could initiate a nuclear attack.

As Thomas Jefferson put it, if the president could be prosecuted, local prosecutors and courts could "bandy him from pillar to post, keep him constantly trudging from north to south and east to west, and withdraw him entirely from his constitutional duties."[1] Worse still, partisan juries might convict the president based on politics rather than actual criminal activity. Even a legitimate conviction would be unacceptable, as the nation cannot function dependably with the president behind bars.

But while granting the president immunity from prosecution while still in office solves one problem, it

risks compromising the sacred principle that no one is above the law. The framers resolved this dilemma with a two-part approach. First, the Constitution provides a discrete means of dealing with a president's intolerable misconduct—*impeachment*. This process does not require the president's presence and, more important, cannot result in his or her incarceration: The Constitution specifies that the only punishment upon conviction in an impeachment trial is loss of office (and, potentially, disqualification from future office). However, it allows that presidents can face criminal punishment once removed from office, thus assuring that they not remain above the law.

The impeachment process, taking place on the floors of Congress rather than in a courtroom, and not involving criminal penalties, does not fit neatly in our usual categories. As a result, there is ongoing debate regarding whether impeachment is a political or a judicial process.

Some argue that because the sole consequence is loss of office, and the indictment and trial are conducted by the legislative branch, whose members face the voters, the process must be viewed as political. Others counter that during impeachment Congress acts in a judicial capacity and thus must rise above partisan politics. This debate evokes the dueling mantras in the old "tastes great, less filling" beer commercials. A careful reading of the Constitution establishes impeachment as a political *and* judicial process.

If the founders had intended impeachment to be wholly judicial, they would have given the courts the leading role in conducting the trial. In fact, they gave serious thought to having impeachment trials be conducted by the U.S. Supreme Court but decided instead to place that authority in the Senate. Indeed, the framers largely kept the courts out of this process.* Although the Constitution does not say this in so many words, it envisions that

---

* The one exception is that the chief justice presides over the trial, since the vice president, who normally presides over the Senate, would have an obvious conflict of interest. Interestingly, the exact nature of the conflict of interest differs today from the situation at the founding. Today, the vice president might favor the president, who selected him and serves as his partner in office. But under the original Constitution, the person receiving the second highest number of votes for president became vice president, so the president and vice president need not be allies. Under those circumstances, the vice president presiding over an impeachment trial might have been expected to stack the deck against the president, increasing the chance that he or she would ascend to the office.

THOMAS JEFFERSON.
Third President of the United States.

following an impeachment trial, the Senate's verdict is final—not subject to review by any court.

However, to conclude that the process is purely political would be to ignore several of the Constitution's provisions. Prior to an impeachment trial, each senator must take a judicial-like "oath or affirmation" (above and beyond her oath of office) to do justice. The Constitution gives the Senate the power to "*try* all impeachments." Just as trial by the *Senate* is necessarily somewhat political, a *trial* by any institution is necessarily somewhat judicial. So too, the Constitution says that, in an impeachment trial, "no person shall be *convicted*" without a two-thirds vote, and sets forth treason, bribery, and "high crimes and misdemeanors" as bases for removal, again using the concepts and vocabulary of criminal law.

The Constitution, then, establishes a political/judicial hybrid. Assigning impeachment to political actors ensures a substantial political dimension to a judicial-like proceeding. The latter requires the essentials of a trial: It must afford presidents due process, the right to confront evidence against them, and the right to present their own. One aspect of a trial that will *not* be present, however, is perfectly impartial judges. We simply cannot expect senators to be indifferent to all considerations except justice in the case at hand. One asks that of judges, not legislators.

One might respond that the senators are indeed judges during the impeachment trial, but that evokes the riddle favored by President Lincoln: "If you call a tail a leg, how many legs does a horse have? No, not five. Calling a tail a leg doesn't make it one." Calling senators judges cannot undo the reality that they are politicians. Members of Congress routinely communicate with constituents and generally have an eye on their next election (though senators, with longer terms, can afford to be less immediately responsive to public opinion than their counterparts in the House). Moreover, the framers expected that many senators would maintain personal or professional relationships with the president. We do not accept judges and juries having such relationships with the parties to a case.

The partial politicization of impeachment is healthy. That senators will take into account not merely the facts and law but also the best interests of their political party, and themselves, safeguards against overly easy conviction. Ideally they will also take into account the best interests of the nation—something they, more than judges, are conditioned and positioned to consider. Presidents will be removed only when two-thirds of a body that faces the voters determines that they and/or the nation will be better off. Far more often than not, convicting the president will require guilty votes from members of the president's own party, giving the verdict to remove the president more legitimacy.

As noted, the Constitution authorizes impeachment for "treason, bribery, or other high crimes and misdemeanors." Treason and bribery are reasonably clear, but what are high crimes and misdemeanors? The phrase was a term of art imported from British law, but not clearly defined there or here. Gerald Ford, at the time a congressman initiating impeachment proceedings against Supreme Court justice William O. Douglas, offered a famous definition: "An impeachable offense is whatever a majority of the House of Representatives considers it to be at a given moment in history."[2]

Ford was speaking of the impeachment of judges, and clarified that presidents could be impeached only for serious offenses. But that distinction got washed away, and many commentators and politicians over the years have approvingly quoted Ford in the context of presidential impeachment. Even so, they are in one sense correct: The Constitution does not define high crimes and misdemeanors, and neither Congress nor the courts have stepped in to fill that void. But equating an impeachable offense with whatever the House of Representatives declares it to be is misguided if meant to suggest that the president serves at the whim of Congress.

The Constitution does not envision that Congress can remove the president any time it pleases. Rather, by specifying that it can do so only for bribery, treason, or high crimes and misdemeanors, the Constitution implies the opposite: Congress may remove the president only when he or she commits certain improper acts. Which brings us back to the paramount question: What are high crimes and misdemeanors?

We find clues from context, starting with the fact that treason and bribery are the two specified bases for removal. Had the Constitution omitted mention of specific crimes justifying impeachment, no one would have doubted that treason and bribery qualified. So why did the framers bother to name these crimes? Presumably they wished to provide a concrete idea of the nature of the conduct warranting removal. The Constitution defines treason as "levying war against [the United States], or in adhering to their enemies, giving them aid and comfort." It didn't have to define bribery, because everyone knows what that is: to get someone to act in one's favor by a gift of money or other improper inducement. If nothing else, the inclusion of treason and bribery suggests that the framers had in mind *serious* misconduct.

It also suggests that they contemplated offenses that compromise the public good. The president who gives or accepts bribes, like the one who commits treason, allows something to compete with the interests of the United States. Worse, in the case of treason (and sometimes bribery), the national security of the United States is directly attacked or subverted.

Significantly, an earlier draft of the Constitution

cited bribery and treason as the *only* grounds for impeachment. Convention delegate George Mason protested that the grounds for impeachment had to be broadened, because treason and bribery "will not reach many great and dangerous offenses."[3] He proposed adding the catch-all "maladministration." (Mason's motion was seconded by Elbridge Gerry, the Massachusetts delegate whose surname and oddly shaped congressional district—it resembled a salamander—gave rise to the term "gerrymander.") Notwithstanding the fact that many state constitutions at the time included "maladministration" as a basis for impeachment, James Madison, widely proclaimed the father of the Constitution, objected that "so vague a term will be equivalent to a tenure during the pleasure of the Senate."[4] Mason withdrew "maladministration" and replaced it with "high crimes and misdemeanors." Madison agreed and the amended clause passed.

The exchange between the two Virginians provides insight into the framers' thinking on impeachment. They did not regard high crimes and misdemeanors as synonymous with "anything Congress decides is disqualifying"—they rejected "maladministration" precisely because it could be so interpreted. The framers consciously rejected the British model in which Parliament can vote "no confidence" against prime ministers and remove them whenever it believes their administration to be ineffective or misguided.

But the framers did not leave treason and bribery as the only bases for conviction and removal. They added high crimes and misdemeanors in order to encompass other "great and dangerous offenses." They wished to reserve impeachment for major misconduct. The dialogue between Madison and Mason dovetails with the specifying of the particularly serious crimes of treason and bribery.

Their exchange, which took place on September 8, 1787, a little more than a week before the delegates voted to adopt the Constitution, comprised the Convention's sole discussion of high crimes and misdemeanors. *The Federalist*, influential essays by Madison, Alexander Hamilton, and John Jay advocating ratification of the Constitution, also briefly touches on the idea of an impeachable offense. Most significantly, in *Federalist 65* Hamilton writes that the impeachable offense arises from "the abuse or violation of some public trust" and "relate[s] chiefly to injuries done immediately to the society itself."[5]

Hamilton's characterization supports the view that the offense must be serious and implies that it need not be criminal. That view has taken hold. Some targets of impeachment, including Supreme Court Justice Samuel Chase in the nation's early days and President Richard Nixon almost two centuries later, insisted that only criminal conduct may be impeachable, but that notion has been rightly rejected. Suppose the president censored his political opponents or pardoned all criminals from his own party. Such conduct, though not specifically prohibited by any statutes, would clearly warrant impeachment and conviction.

Just as there may be impeachable offenses that are not crimes, some crimes may not be impeachable. Certain offenses, such as traffic violations (were a president ever to get behind the wheel), are too minor to warrant impeachment, even if they technically constitute crimes. No one would approve removing a president because he or she went fishing without a license. The Constitution's reference to "misdemeanors," a legal term referring to minor offenses generally punishable by at most one year in prison, is misleading. The phrase "high crimes and misdemeanors" constitutes a single term. Some commentators interpret the modifier "high" to apply to both "crime" and "misdemeanors" and thus to reinforce that only serious misconduct qualifies. Others believe that "misdemeanors" was included simply to clarify that impeachment did not require an actual crime. While we don't know exactly how the framers regarded "high crimes and misdemeanors," the inclusion of misdemeanors does not imply that minor misconduct may suffice for impeachment. All the evidence suggests that only major misconduct qualifies.

Focusing on the above considerations, including Hamilton's reference to "the abuse or violation of some public trust," we may be tempted to generalize that an impeachable offense involves conduct, whether or not criminal, that undercuts the legitimacy of the United States government. However, some behavior seemingly outside that definition must be impeachable. A president who commits armed robbery or murder in a purely private setting cannot remain in office. Certain actions, even if unrelated to official responsibilities, are simply too egregious to allow the president to maintain the necessary public trust.

But apart from such rare exceptions, the rule seems to be that high crimes and misdemeanors will typically involve an abuse of the presidential office itself. At times, this standard is easy to apply, as when Richard Nixon misused various government agencies and thereby transgressed his Article II powers. At other times, the situation is less clear. Defenders of Bill Clinton argued that lying about his sexual relationship with a White House intern did not constitute an impeachable offense because it did not involve a public matter. Opponents countered that perjury undermines the ability of the judicial system to function and thus compromises the legitimacy of United States government.

We cannot know how the framers would have regarded the Clinton affair. When they used vague or general language such as "high crimes and misdemeanors," we must look beyond some original understanding (if any there be) of the text. That may be healthy, particularly in the context of impeachment. What was regarded as a grievous offense in 1787 will not necessarily be so viewed today, and vice versa.

It does not follow that we should ignore the framers' views or values. They bequeathed us a brilliant Constitution, the text of which represents the starting (and sometimes ending) point of every constitutional question. Where their thinking can be discerned, we benefit from their wisdom. But we often need to look further, seeing what lessons can be gleaned from subsequent history.

GEORGE T. BROWN, SERGEANT-AT-ARMS OF THE SENATE, SERVING THE SUMMONS ON PRESIDENT JOHNSON.—Sketched by T. R. Davis.—[See Page 195.]

T W O

ANDREW JOHNSON
SURVIVES

Andrew Johnson's presidency was born in crisis. The Tennessean became the United States' 17th president upon the assassination of Abraham Lincoln on April 14, 1865. He had been selected as Lincoln's running mate by the Republican Convention in June 1864, replacing the sitting vice president, Hannibal Hamlin.

In making this unusual move, which Lincoln privately endorsed, the party sought to bridge two divides: Unlike Lincoln, a Republican from a Union state, Johnson was a Democrat from a Confederate state. As the only United States senator from a secessionist state to remain in Congress (until Lincoln appointed him military governor of Tennessee), rather than resign and join the Confederacy, and having openly denounced secession as treason, Johnson had credibility with Republicans and his presence on the ticket figured to attract Southerners and Northern pro-war Democrats. He and Lincoln campaigned not under the banner of the Republican Party but as the National Union Party, and won election easily in November.

Johnson's tenure as vice president got off to a shaky start. He showed up at the inauguration drunk, and did nothing to conceal this condition during his long and rambling speech. The reputation of the rough-hewn, uneducated Johnson never fully recovered, though the ever-conciliatory Lincoln forgave his partner the transgression, calling it "a severe lesson for Andy, but I do not think he will do it again."[1] Johnson justified Lincoln's faith, serving him loyally and serving his purpose as a unifying figure.

But if Johnson's term as vice president promoted unity, his ascendancy to the presidency had the opposite effect. For Republicans, devastated by Lincoln's assassination to begin with, it was a bitter pill to see the opposition party handed the White House just five years after the Republicans had attained it for the first time. It made matters much worse that the new Democratic president didn't share their vision on the major issue of the day, an issue at the heart of a recently concluded war that had claimed 620,000 lives.

The so-called Radical Republicans, who controlled both houses of Congress, saw little room for compromise when it came to racial justice. They thought Lincoln's plan for Reconstruction insufficiently aggressive, but they admired his steadfast prosecution of the Civil War and expected to work with him in its aftermath. They planned to condition the return of Confederate states to the Union on those states' willingness to give black men full political rights. Following Lincoln's assassination, the Republicans suddenly had to deal with an openly white supremacist president who had been a slaveholder and lacked Republicans' vision of Reconstruction.

Initially, Andrew Johnson seemed accommodating. He kept Lincoln's cabinet, and sounded conciliatory notes about his intention to work with Congress across party lines. Even ardent abolitionists such as Charles Sumner, the militant Massachusetts senator, pronounced themselves pleased with the new president. To be sure, not all Republicans shared that view. Some, including members of Congress, believed Johnson complicit in Lincoln's assassination. It didn't take long for major divisions to develop between Johnson and those Republicans who initially gave him the benefit of the doubt.

Johnson favored extending the vote to literate, tax-paying freedmen, but maintained that "it would not do to let the Negro have universal suffrage now; it would breed a war of races."[2] He insisted the matter be left to the states, a position anathema to the Radical Republicans, who wished to deny reentry into the Union to any states that refused to give black men full voting rights. Naturally, Johnson also opposed a more far-reaching proposed constitutional amendment, a forerunner to the 14th Amendment, requiring states to give black people equal protection of the laws. He also vetoed a bill extending the Freedmen's Bureau, which assisted former slaves, as well as a Civil Rights Act, which defined national citizenship to include African Americans and gave them various rights, such as acquiring property, making contracts, and testifying in court. Johnson pardoned countless Confederate leaders over the objections of the Radical Republicans.

The division within the federal government mirrored and exacerbated divisions in the country at large. Race riots broke out. In several states, including Johnson's home state of Tennessee, mobs of white men killed dozens of black people. Predictably, Johnson and the Radical Republicans each blamed the other for the violence.

In the fall of 1866, Johnson traveled the country (his so-called "swing around the circle") to make a series of inflammatory speeches attacking Congress. Radical Republicans returned the favor, refusing even to refer to Johnson as the President. Instead, he was "The Acting President," "His Accidency" or "His Vulgarity." Republicans won the battle for public opinion. In the midterm elections that November, the Radical Republicans substantially increased their majorities in both houses of Congress.

They almost immediately sought to exploit their growing power. In January 1867, triggered by another controversial Johnson veto, this one of a bill giving black men the vote in the District of Columbia, the House Judiciary Committee commenced an investigation into Johnson's conduct with an eye toward impeachment.

The long investigation included an extensive effort to locate an allegedly treasonous letter from then-Governor Johnson to Jefferson Davis, president of the Confederate States of America, but it turned out that the letter did not exist. The committee also pursued evidence that Johnson was part of the conspiracy to assassinate Lincoln. At its final hearing, 10 months later, the committee called as a witness one of its own members, Ohio congressman James Mitchell Ashley, who claimed to have evidence, which he failed to produce, implicating Johnson in the Lincoln assassination. Under skeptical questioning by Democratic congressmen, Ashley acknowledged that he believed that several presidents had been poisoned by their vice presidents (successfully in the cases of Zachary Taylor and William Henry Harrison).

The threat of impeachment did not faze President Johnson, whose considerable flaws did not include timidity. After meeting Johnson, no less an authority on character than novelist Charles Dickens declared him "a man not to be turned or trifled with. A man (I should say) who must be killed to be got out of the way."[3] The leading Radical Republicans matched Johnson's determination, setting them on a collision course with him.

Throughout 1867, the chasm between Congress and the president widened. Congress passed the Reconstruction Act to give the federal government power to suspend state officials who impeded Reconstruction and to require former Confederate states to hold constitutional conventions dedicated to establishing racial equality. Johnson vetoed the bill; Congress overrode the veto. This was the first of 15 Johnson vetoes to be overridden, an event which until then was practically nonexistent. For the preceding 16 presidents, only two had vetoes overridden.

President Ulysses S. Grant

The total number of overrides before Johnson was six. His total of 15 remains unequaled to this day, even though he served less than one term.

The most consequential battle between Congress and the Johnson White House involved the Tenure of Office Act, which required the president to get the Senate's consent before removing any officials whose appointment required Senate confirmation. This measure could lock in place Johnson's cabinet, all members of which were Lincoln carryovers, some of whom supported Congress's aggressive approach to Reconstruction. Moreover, the Tenure of Office Act specified that failure to abide by its terms constituted a crime as well as "high misdemeanor." It was, in other words, impeachment bait. Congress passed it on February 18, 1867, and Johnson vetoed it on March 2. Congress overrode the veto the next day.

The new law posed no immediate issue, but over time Johnson grew wary of some members of his cabinet, especially Secretary of War Edwin Stanton. Stanton sided—and perhaps colluded—with the Radical Republicans in most of their battles with Johnson. On August 12, Johnson suspended Stanton while Congress was in recess, and appointed General Ulysses S. Grant as an interim replacement. Stanton replied to notification of his suspension by claiming that the Tenure of Office Act protected him from removal, but in light of Grant's acceptance of the interim position, "I have no alternative but to submit, under protest, to superior force."[4]

Meanwhile, after its wide-ranging investigation, in November the House Judiciary Committee, by a 5–4 vote, passed out of committee a resolution to impeach President Johnson. The yes votes were cast by Radical Republicans, with two moderate Republicans and two Democrats opposed. The majority report located impeachable offenses primarily in Johnson's improper use of his veto power and pardon power. A dissenting report by the two Republicans stated dissatisfaction with Johnson's policies but claimed the absence of any impeachable offenses. The Democrats' dissenting report praised Johnson for protecting the United States from internal enemies.

The resolution went to the full House in December. After very limited debate—just two speeches on each side—the House rejected impeachment overwhelmingly by vote of 108–57. Opponents of the resolution successfully argued that Johnson could not be impeached since no crime on his part was even alleged.

In the meantime, much background maneuvering took place with respect to Johnson's suspension of Stanton. The Tenure of Office Act appeared to require

Johnson to get the Senate's consent before discharging Stanton, but he had only suspended him, not discharged him, and Congress had not been in session. On January 10, 1868, General Grant informed Johnson that, if the Senate did not concur in Stanton's suspension, he would resign his interim appointment. A few days later, the Senate passed a resolution instructing the president to reinstate Stanton. Four days later, Grant abandoned his office and Stanton returned to it.

On February 21, 1868, President Johnson fired Stanton and replaced him with Major General Lorenzo Thomas, a well-regarded career military man. That evening, the Senate adopted a resolution declaring that Johnson lacked the authority to take these actions. Three days later, the House voted 126–47, by straight party vote, to impeach the president. Meanwhile, Stanton hunkered down in his office in the War Department and had Thomas arrested by federal marshals. After posting $5,000 bail, Thomas marched over to what he considered his rightful office, only to be rebuffed by Stanton. A frustrated Thomas retreated to the White House to inform Johnson of the stalemate.

A House select committee quickly drafted and approved nine articles of impeachment pertaining to the firing and attempted replacement of Stanton. The committee rejected an article proposed by Massachusetts congressman Benjamin Butler concerning the incendiary speeches President Johnson made the previous year. The full House then adopted the nine articles and appointed

THE LAST SPEECH ON IMPEACHMENT—THADDEUS STEVENS CLOSING THE DEBATE IN THE HOUSE, MARCH 2.—[SKETCHED BY T. R. DAVIS.]

seven "managers" to serve as the prosecution team during Johnson's trial in the Senate. Butler, one of the managers, persuaded his House colleagues to reconsider and adopt the proposed tenth article. It said that Johnson's speeches violated "the dignities and proprieties" of his office and destroyed the "harmonies and courtesies which ought to exist and be maintained between the executive and legislative branches."

Leading abolitionist Thaddeus Stevens proposed an eleventh article, which reiterated the charges in the other articles and added allegations based on a speech Johnson made in August 1866 supposedly asserting that Congress lacked the power to make laws (because it was a Congress of only some states) or propose constitutional amendments. Article 11 of the articles of impeachment declared that, by promoting his deficient understanding of the Constitution, Johnson dishonored his oath to faithfully defend it. The new article also passed overwhelmingly.

On March 5, 1868, the Senate commenced the first presidential impeachment trial in U.S. history. Indeed, there had been just a handful of prior impeachments of any federal officials, and only a single conviction. That case merits an asterisk in the historical record: Judge West Humphreys, impeached and convicted for joining the Confederacy, had long abandoned his post and did not appear at his trial or contest his prosecution. Humphreys was tried in absentia and found guilty after a trial that lasted a single afternoon.

The chief justice presiding over the trial of Andrew Johnson was Salmon P. Chase, which illustrates that foresight by the drafters of the Constitution could do only so much to ward off problems. They provided that the chief justice would preside over a president's impeachment trial in order to avoid the vice president's conflict of interest. But Chase was a presidential wannabe who had sought the office in 1860. President Lincoln selected him as secretary of the treasury (and later appointed him to the Court) as part of his "team of rivals," but kept a careful eye on his ambitious underling. Lincoln correctly surmised that Chase would never relinquish his desire to be president. Even as he presided over Andrew Johnson's

The Senate as a court of impeachment for the trial of President Andrew Johnson. Sketched in 1868 by Theodore R. Davis.

impeachment trial, Chase was angling for the Democratic presidential nomination—surely an easier task if the incumbent president was removed. So much for avoiding conflict of interest.

Yet one cannot assume that Chase wished to see Johnson convicted, and some perceived otherwise. On March 4, the eve of the trial, Chase hosted a reception at his home and Johnson made an appearance. Newspaper reports of his attendance rankled anti-Johnson partisans.

Chase was hardly the only participant in Johnson's trial whose impartiality was questioned. The senators to try the case included Chase's son-in-law, William Sprague (from Rhode Island), and Johnson's son-in-law, David

Patterson (Tennessee). While few registered complaints about their involvement, the participation of Ohio's Benjamin Wade, the president pro tempore of the Senate, became a major source of contention.

If Johnson were removed from office, Wade would assume the presidency. The Constitution failed to provide for the circumstance of the vice president succeeding to the presidency and leaving the vice presidency vacant—a problem not fixed until adoption of the 25th Amendment a century later. Thus, when Andrew Johnson became president upon Lincoln's assassination, the vice presidency stood vacant. Meanwhile, a founding-era statute put the president pro tempore next in the line of presidential succession.

It was no accident that Wade, a bold leader of the Radical Republicans, occupied the office of president pro tempore. When it became vacant in March 1867 upon the departure of a senator defeated in the November 1866 election, everyone knew that the Senate's new president pro tempore could soon end up in the White House. The House of Representatives had already attempted to impeach Johnson once, and had by no means given up on the idea. For that reason, the Republican-dominated Senate chose Wade over fellow senators considered too moderate for the taste of the Radical Republicans. Wade mildly protested that he was not suited for the job ("I am no parliamentarian"),[5] knowing full well that his colleagues had in mind for him a different job down the line. Indeed, Wade supposedly had his future cabinet picked out.

To complicate all the potential conflicts of interest, Chief Justice Chase was believed to be hostile toward Wade and therefore inclined to tip the scales toward acquittal.

The swearing in of the senators by Chase on March 5 proceeded alphabetically, which meant most of the senators had been sworn in by the time Wade stepped up. Before he could take the oath, Democrats rose to object that his conflict of interest should disqualify Wade from participation in the trial. The Senate halted the swearing-in process to take up the question. More than 20 senators weighed in. Those who defended Wade's involvement pressed the point that Andrew Johnson's own son-in-law would be among the senators deciding the case. Ohio's John Sherman, the younger brother of the great General William Tecumseh Sherman, argued that to remove his fellow Ohioan would deprive their state of full representation at the trial.

At the completion of the arguments, Chief Justice Chase deferred decision: Because the Senate had yet to be constituted as a "court" for the purposes of the trial, any determination about Wade was premature. The Senate voted narrowly, 24–20, to support Chase's punt, and Wade took the oath the following day, March 6, with no guarantee that he would remain on the case.

Following the completion of the oaths, the House managers and Johnson's four defense attorneys made their first appearance. The latter included Benjamin Curtis, a former justice of the Supreme Court who wrote a dissenting opinion in the infamous *Dred Scott* case and resigned from the Court (partly in protest) shortly thereafter. Curtis, defending a president accused of obstructing the push for racial equality, had strong credentials as a supporter of civil rights.

The defense demanded that they be given an additional 40 days to answer the impeachment charges. "Forty days!" thundered Benjamin Butler, an avowed enemy of the president. "As long as it took God to destroy the world by a flood!"[6] The Senate deliberated over the request in private for two hours before deciding to grant the defense 10 days.

No one was overjoyed with the compromise, and tempers flared. The defense attorneys objected to the Senate's "railroad speed" in conducting the trial, a charge that resonated in those early days of rail travel. But not everyone thought the pace too fast. Future president James Garfield, then a member of the House, later bemoaned that the trial was hostage to "the insane love of speaking among public men" and that the proceedings sank in a marsh of endless "words, words, words."[7]

Andrew Johnson's formal response to the charges came on its due date, March 23, and set forth a detailed description of the president's actions, the legal authority behind them, and his motives. The next day, the House managers offered a boilerplate one-paragraph written reply. They expressed their objections more passionately in statements on the Senate floor. Butler declared that "the President is as guilty of malfeasance and misdemeanor in office as ever man was guilty of malfeasance or misdemeanor in office since nations began to be upon the earth."[8] He took particular issue with Johnson's claim that he could disregard the Tenure of Office Act because it violated the Constitution. The president was claiming "power thus to lay hands upon the Constitution of the country and rend it in tatters."[9]

The senators also took up the issue of timing again. Johnson's team had requested another thirty-day continuance. After some angry back-and-forth, the Senate compromised on a six-day continuance.

The trial began in earnest at 1:00 p.m. on March 30, before a full gallery that included the British novelist Anthony Trollope. Butler made the opening statement for the managers. The very fact that he was selected to do so reflected the Republicans' mood. A charismatic, controversial Union general, Butler gained notoriety during the military occupation of New Orleans. His heavy-handed administration of the city included seizing a 38-piece set of silverware from a woman attempting to cross Union lines illegally, earning him the sobriquet "Spoons." Benjamin "Spoons" Butler was among the most outspoken and militant opponents of Andrew Johnson. He apparently adhered to the batty view that Johnson had acted in concert with John Wilkes Booth and others to assassinate President Lincoln.

Reading his three-hour opening statement, Butler emphasized that an actual crime is not necessary for conviction by the Senate. He instructed senators that they were "a law unto yourselves, bound only by the natural principles of equity and justice."[10] He defended Senator Wade's participation in the trial, the issue deferred by Chief Justice Chase and still unresolved.* Butler argued that the Senate is not a court, and therefore judicial rules such as those regarding conflict of interest have no place.

After addressing various legal and factual issues surrounding Johnson's alleged violation of the Tenure of Office Act, Butler finally got around to the article of impeachment that was his personal baby—Article 10, based on Johnson's inflammatory speeches. But that charge may have rung hollow coming from Butler, whose own rhetorical excesses were on display toward the end of his diatribe: "This man by murder most foul succeeded to the presidency, and is the elect of an assassin to that high office, and not of the people."[11] Butler closed even more melodramatically: "The future political welfare and liberties of all men hang trembling on the decision of the hour."[12]

The managers' presentation of evidence, consisting of both documents and live witnesses, lasted six days, though one full day was consumed by the question of the chief justice's authority to rule on disputes over evidence. After Chase made a ruling on challenged testimony, the House managers protested that he had no power to make

---

* Wade abstained from voting throughout the trial, until a key motion right before the actual vote to acquit or convict. He voted on that motion and on the articles of impeachment themselves. Perhaps because the outcome did not end up turning on his vote, no one renewed the objection to his participation.

such determinations. They preferred that disputes be resolved by the Senate, where Republicans enjoyed a comfortable majority. However, after much debate the Senate elected not to disqualify Chase from such rulings.

Most of the managers' case involved setting forth the factual record surrounding the Tenure of Office Act and Johnson's dismissal of Stanton, though they also called to testify several reporters who had witnessed the inflammatory speeches that gave rise to Article 10 of the articles of impeachment. During cross-examination of these reporters, Johnson's attorneys elicited that the president appeared sober during these speeches, undermining Republicans' efforts to present him as a lush.

The managers reserved for the end a clever touch, introducing into evidence two lists: a long list of all cabinet heads ever appointed by presidents and a shorter list of all such cabinet heads whom presidents discharged. The latter included a single name—Timothy Pickering, whom John Adams dismissed as secretary of state in 1800. For good measure, the managers introduced into evidence the correspondence of Adams and Pickering that demonstrated Pickering's blatant insubordination. Thus the only cabinet dismissal prior to Johnson's firing of Stanton took place under extreme circumstances. The managers suggested that, even apart from violating the Tenure of Office Act, Johnson's dismissal of a cabinet secretary was un-American.

The defense requested, and over strong objections was granted, a five-day adjournment. They began their case on Thursday, April 9, with Ben Curtis's opening statement. Unlike his counterpart Butler, a fellow Massachusetts attorney, Curtis spoke without notes. He advanced three related claims: 1) Stanton was not covered by the Tenure of Office Act;* 2) any misconduct by the president was unintentional, since he genuinely believed that Stanton was not covered by the Act; 3) if Stanton *was* covered, the Act was unconstitutional, and Johnson was right not to abide by it.

Curtis also went after Butler's claim that the Senate was a law unto itself, free to convict a president even if he violated no laws. If that were so, Curtis argued, then U.S. citizens' constitutional protections against ex post facto laws (laws punishing behavior that was legal at the time committed) and bills of attainder (laws singling out people for punishment without trial) somehow did not apply to presidents. And he assailed Article 10, which based impeachment on Johnson's speeches, as an obvious affront to freedom of speech.

Next came the parade of defense witnesses, who mostly set forth their versions of how Johnson acted in response to the Tenure of Office Act, with an emphasis on his good motives. The managers' frequent objections to

---

* The technical question whether the Act applied to Stanton consumed a fair amount of the trial. The Act stated that it protected cabinet members from discharge "during the term of the president by whom they may have been appointed and one more thereafter." The key term was . . . "term." Had Lincoln's term expired with his death? Or did it continue until its natural expiration in 1869?

the admissibility of this line of testimony created lengthy disputes that prompted Republican senator Charles Sumner to make a radical suggestion: Thenceforth all questions that were not obviously irrelevant should be permitted. Sumner's motion cut against his own side, but he had grown impatient because he regarded Johnson's guilt as a foregone conclusion. Who needed all the legal wrangling? But Sumner's proposal to facilitate the trial was defeated.

An adjournment was granted during the defense case when one of Johnson's counsel took ill, prompting Butler to fume that, while the trial dragged on, "Our fellow citizens are being murdered day by day. There is not a man here who does not know that the moment justice is done on this great criminal, these murders will cease."[13] Butler laid the blame for racist lynchings perpetrated by the Ku Klux Klan (formed just three years earlier) at the doorstep of the Oval Office.

When the trial resumed, the defense called a potentially crucial witness, Secretary of the Navy Gideon Welles. Welles planned to testify that the cabinet had advised Johnson that the Tenure of Office Act was unconstitutional, supporting the notion that Johnson's noncompliance with the Act was in good faith. The managers objected that such testimony was irrelevant. The two sides strenuously argued the point, and Chief Justice Chase ruled the testimony admissible because it went to the president's intent. However, by 29–20 vote, the Senate reversed the ruling, thus gutting a major defense claim.

The Senate also reversed Chase's ruling allowing Welles to testify that Johnson had been advised by his cabinet that Stanton was not covered by the Tenure of Office Act. As a result of the two rulings, Welles stepped down and the defense didn't bother calling the secretaries of state, treasury, and interior, all of whom were expected to corroborate Welles's testimony.

The defense case concluded on April 20. Though 41 witnesses had testified for the two sides (25 for the prosecution, 16 for the defense), no significant factual disputes emerged. What separated the sides were legal technicalities and one overarching question: Assuming President Johnson lacked the authority to fire and re-place Secretary Stanton, did those wrongful acts rise to the level of high crimes and misdemeanors justifying his removal from office?

The closing arguments by the two sides commenced on April 22 and did not conclude until May 4. Much of the arguments by the eight counsel—four for each side—revolved around the legal and constitutional nuances sur-rounding the Tenure of Office Act, presented in every conceivable light. Even if all these questions were to be resolved in favor of the managers, however, the propriety of conviction did not necessarily follow. Indeed, the man-agers knew they were on shaky ground in claiming that any particular actions by Johnson amounted to impeach-able offenses. They at times subtly and at times not so subtly changed the indictment to something more global: Andrew Johnson was a power-hungry monster.

House manager George Boutwell, an abolitionist from Massachusetts who would become secretary of the treasury in President Grant's administration, claimed Johnson pursued his enemies "with all the violence of his personal hatred."[14] Boutwell also portrayed Johnson as a white supremacist who planned to keep blacks in chains. The president's resistance to Reconstruction amounted to a criminal scheme to subvert the government and disgraced America in the eyes of civilized nations. Boutwell also tethered his broadsides against Johnson to Article 10 of the articles of impeachment. Johnson's incendiary speeches showed him to be unfit for the office.

The defense felt compelled to defend the president not only against the articles of impeachment, but also as president and person. Johnson's attorney and close personal friend, Thomas A.R. Nelson, reminded everyone of his client's opposition to secession and lamented that one who imperiled himself to fight treason was now stigmatized as a traitor himself. Johnson's opposition to the Republicans' aggressive Reconstruction plan stemmed from his desire to heal a wounded country. Nelson added ruefully that "if he erred in this, it was almost a divine error."[15]

It seemed impossible that Boutwell and Nelson were describing the same person. The man Boutwell depicted as a hateful would-be tyrant was, according to Nelson, a man of unsurpassed integrity and only the purest motives.

Defense counsel William Groesbeck, who had served as a law clerk for Chief Justice Chase, echoed the notion that if Johnson went wrong with respect to

Reconstruction, it was from his yearning for national reconciliation and his absence of malice toward the South. Groesbeck was followed by manager Thaddeus Stevens. The great abolitionist was so infirm that partway through his statement he gave his draft to Butler to read out loud. Butler must have enjoyed the task, as Stevens's speech contained outlandish rhetoric to rival his own. Though never quite charging that Johnson conspired with John Wilkes Booth, Stevens linked the two men. Johnson was an "offspring of assassination" who could not escape the "just vengeance of the law."[16]

Thomas Williams, a congressman from Pennsylvania, went even further than his fellow managers in impugning the president's integrity. He was the only manager to cast aspersions on Johnson's opposition to secession, suggesting that it was undertaken solely from political opportunism. He opined that if Johnson were acquitted, no president would ever be impeached, no matter how egregious his misconduct.

Before the next attorney could take his turn, Butler rose to attack defense counsel Nelson for raising an argument that Butler considered irrelevant and offensive. Nelson responded, "So far as any concern that the gentleman desires to make of a personal character with me is concerned, this is not the place to make it. Let him make it elsewhere, if he desires to do it."[17] This challenge prompted Sumner to call for formal condemnation of Nelson for trying to provoke a duel. Nelson replied that while "not a duelist by profession," he would not back down if challenged.[18] (Incredibly, dueling was still accepted in parts of the United States in the 1860s, including Nelson's home state of Tennessee.) The Senate rejected Sumner's proposed censure of Nelson by a vote of 35–10.

Next came the closing argument of defense counsel William Evarts, a brilliant attorney destined to become Johnson's attorney general after the trial and secretary of state under President Rutherford B. Hayes. Evarts spoke eloquently, and spoke and spoke and spoke—for almost four days. He belabored all the technical legal points, but also emphasized the extraordinary nature of impeachment and the need to heed the views of the American people concerning its usage. Evarts characterized impeachment as "this power which has lain in the Constitution like a sword in its sheath."[19] Now that it was drawn, ordinary folks wished to know what crime the president stood accused of. Evarts proceeded to riff on the public's "wish to know," caricaturing the impeachers in the process:

> [The People] wish to know whether the President has betrayed our liberties or our possessions to a foreign state. They wish to know whether he has delivered up a fortress or surrendered a fleet. They wish to know whether he has made merchandise of the public trust and turned authority to private gain. And when informed that none of these things are charged, imputed, or even declaimed about, they yet seek

further information and are told that he has removed a member of his cabinet.[20]

Evarts proceeded to tutor his audience in realpoli-
tik. The president's problems stemmed from 1) having
attained office through an assassin's bullets rather than
the people's ballots, and 2) the opposition party domi-
nating Congress. Johnson was impeached solely because
of those circumstances and not because he did anything
remotely warranting that drastic remedy. Not wishing to
waste an opportunity, Republicans contrived "to make
out a crime, a fault, a danger that should enlist the terrible machinery of impeachment and condemnation."[21]
Put differently, Republicans impeached Johnson simply
because they could. Near the end of his exhaustive ora-
tion, Evarts succinctly summarized the situation: "It is all
political. All these thunder clouds are political."[22]

Next up was Henry Stanbery, Johnson's attorney
general until he stepped down to join Johnson's defense
team at the trial. (His reward would be a nomination by
Johnson to the U.S. Supreme Court; his punishment, the
Senate's refusal to confirm him.) Stanbery, like co-coun-
sel Nelson and Groesback, vouched for the president's
character, suggesting that in this regard Johnson was the
equal of George Washington.

The final closing statement, by manager John Bingham of Ohio, was much anticipated because of Bingham's
exalted reputation as an orator. (He would later earn ac-
claim as a driving force behind the 14th Amendment.)

With little left to be said, however, Bingham repeated and summarized the arguments of his colleagues. He did close with a stirring peroration, pleading on behalf of "the violated majesty of the law, by the graves of a half-million of martyred hero-patriots who made death beautiful by the sacrifice of themselves for their country, the Constitution and the laws, and who, by their sublime example, have taught us that all must obey the law; that none are above the law, that no man lives for himself alone, but each for all."[23] Though perhaps more poetic than logical, his words were met with a prolonged standing ovation.

The managers' case suffered serious flaws. While most of the articles of impeachment stemmed from Johnson's discharge of Stanton, several specifically involved his replacement of Stanton with an interim director. Statutes dating back to 1792 authorized the president to make such interim appointments, and the question as to whether a later statute effectively repealed those statutes seemed highly technical. As noted, a second technical question concerned whether the Tenure of Office Act even applied to Stanton.

An overriding question presented itself with respect to these legal disputes: Could disagreement about nuanced legal matters possibly be the basis for conviction and removal of a president? To the extent that the debate on the Senate floor resembled a panel of law professors offering competing interpretations of a statute, by its very nature it did not concern an impeachable offense.

Johnson was at most wrong, but not so heinously wrong as to justify the political death penalty.

That perspective also applied to the dispute at the heart of the controversy: the constitutionality of the Tenure of Office Act. Johnson took the plausible position that, insofar as it prevented presidents from discharging their cabinet members without the Senate's consent, the Act violated the Constitution. Subsequent history validates this position. Congress repealed the Tenure of Office Act in 1887, and the Supreme Court deemed a similar law unconstitutional in 1926.

As a matter of policy, the idea of forcing a president to live with cabinet members he considers insubordinate or incompetent is problematic. In any event, a president must interpret the Constitution as he or she thinks proper. If the president and Congress clash over different interpretations, the solution is to turn to the third branch—the courts, the ultimate interpreters of the Constitution. Had the Supreme Court held that Johnson could not fire Stanton, and had he disobeyed their decision, then and only then would there be grounds for impeachment.

The managers rejected that position, starting with Butler's opening statement. He acknowledged the indisputable fact that a president may disagree with Congress about the constitutionality of a law. The president's remedy, though, is to veto the bill. Once a veto is overridden, he must execute the law. He refuses to do so, said Butler, "at his peril [and] that peril is impeachment."[24]

Why shouldn't Johnson instead refuse to abide by

the law and allow the courts to resolve the issue? Butler had no good answer, but he did have a fallback position: Even if that were a legitimate course of action, Johnson had not undertaken it. He had done nothing to submit the constitutionality of the Tenure of Office Act to the courts.

The managers were on shaky ground here. For one thing, Johnson had in fact wanted the Supreme Court to resolve the matter and had hoped that would occur when Stanton had Thomas arrested for accepting the appointment as his replacement. Thomas testified that, when he informed Johnson of his arrest, the president expressed satisfaction because he wanted the matter resolved by the courts. It was the Republicans, not Johnson, who saw to it that charges against Thomas were dropped so the constitutionality of the Act would not be adjudicated. Besides, why was Johnson obliged to take the matter to court? Why not act as he thought appropriate and let the aggrieved party (in this case Stanton or a member of Congress) bring suit to challenge him? That was and is the normal course.

Once again, even if one saw that matter differently— if one felt that the president must enforce the law until the courts rule in his favor—this was a debatable matter that separated constitutional lawyers of good faith. Error on such a matter could not justify impeachment.

The two articles of impeachment based on speeches by Johnson ran into a different difficulty. No official transcripts of those speeches existed, and there were conflicting accounts of just what Johnson had said. But quite apart from that, to base impeachment on speeches, even if they were considered outrageous or erroneous, violated the spirit if not letter of the First Amendment.

If the arguments favored acquittal, arithmetic favored conviction: 42 of the 54 senators were Republicans, so a party-line vote in this partisan atmosphere would doom the president. The run-up to the day of decision witnessed the sort of politicking that takes place before any important congressional vote: meetings, negotiations, deals, arm-twisting among the senators and party leaders, as well as senators hearing from their constituents. President Johnson, for his part, let the Republicans know his intention to reward an acquittal by appointing a new secretary of war to their liking.

On May 11, the Senate deliberated behind closed doors for 15 hours, recessing only for dinner. Before debating whether to convict and remove President Johnson, they took up a series of procedural questions. One interesting issue illustrates how the Constitution leaves open the conduct of the impeachment trial. The Constitution specifies that conviction brings mandatory removal from office, and sets forth an optional additional punishment: disqualification from future office. If Johnson were convicted and removed, could he run in the forthcoming presidential election (or for any office thereafter)? The Senate would have to decide, but by what margin? The Constitution says two-thirds is required for conviction, but is silent about the vote needed to impose the additional punishment of future disqualification. A good argument could be made for either two-thirds or a mere majority. The senators debated this issue but failed to resolve it. They would have to take it up again if and when the president was convicted.

This and other issues, and the merits of the 11 articles of impeachment, kept the senators busy until midnight. A final vote on the articles was deferred until May 16. On that fateful day, more than 1,500 spectators crammed in to a Senate gallery that comfortably accommodated one thousand. Those present would uniformly report electricity in the air. People understood that they were about to witness something unprecedented and history-making.

At noon, Chief Justice Chase gaveled the proceedings to begin. Senator George Williams from Oregon, one of the most pro-conviction members, proposed that Article 11 (the omnibus article believed to command the most support) be voted on first, and the senators agreed. One by one each of the 54 senators was called, rose, and announced his vote. (Two were so infirm that Chase gave them permission to remain seated, but they rose nevertheless.) Thirty-five voted to convict and 19 to acquit— one vote short of the two-thirds required for conviction.

Williams again sprang up, this time to ask for a 15-minute recess, presumably to allow the pro-conviction forces to regroup. When this unorthodox proposal received no support, he moved for a 10-day adjournment. Chase overruled the motion but the Senate, by vote of 32–21, reversed the ruling.

During that ten-day break, anti-Johnson forces both

inside and outside the Senate desperately sought to pressure the seven Republicans who had voted to acquit. The Republican Party's national convention met to nominate a presidential candidate and, in addition to nominating Ulysses S. Grant, expressed its support for the conviction of President Johnson. The party platform declared Johnson guilty of high crimes and misdemeanors. The Republican senators who days earlier voted to acquit on Article 11 were (in absentia) alternately vilified and beseeched to vote differently on the outstanding articles.

The outcome remained uncertain when the Senate reassembled as an impeachment court on May 26. The senators discussed and rejected a notion to adjourn for another month. It was then moved and approved to skip Article 1, which had little chance, and vote on Articles 2 and 3, which, dealing with the replacement of Edwin Stanton rather than his discharge, supposedly had more support. This presumed, oddly, that some senators thought Johnson had the power to fire Stanton but not to designate a replacement. As it happens, all 54 senators voted the same way on Article 2 as they had on Article 11. Once again, Johnson escaped conviction by a single vote.

The vote on Article 3 produced déjà vu all over again—the same 35 to convict and 19 to acquit. At this point the defeated anti-Johnson forces adopted an exit strategy: declare victory and go home. Charles Sumner proclaimed that despite the nominal acquittal, the Senate had delivered a profound moral judgment against

Johnson. By a vote of 34–16, the Senate disbanded the trial without voting on the remaining eight articles.

Later that day, Stanton notified Johnson by letter that he would abandon his office. Other opponents of the president were slower to accept defeat. Congress immediately launched an investigation into reports that some of the Republican votes to acquit were secured by bribes. Thaddeus Stevens, clinging to life, immediately drafted new articles of impeachment. None of these efforts bore fruit, although Stevens shared his proposed articles in his valedictory speech on the Senate floor on July 7. The lifelong devotee of racial justice also proclaimed that the nation would not be truly blessed until everyone accepted that all human beings enjoy the same inalienable rights.

The seven Republicans who voted to acquit Johnson earned the title "Seven Tall Men" but paid a price for their courage: None was reelected to the Senate. One of them, Edmund Ross, appeared to support conviction but changed his mind late in the process. Ross later wrote that as he cast his vote, "I almost literally looked down into my open grave."[25] He received posthumous glory, meriting a chapter in John F. Kennedy's book *Profiles in Courage*, which called his vote the most heroic act in U.S. history. Alas, some evidence suggests that Ross received a bribe from pro-Johnson forces.

Andrew Johnson served out the remaining nine months of his term as a man without a party. He had abandoned the Democrats to join Lincoln's ticket, yet never became a Republican and alienated Republicans by opposing

Reconstruction. He did not actively seek reelection as president, though he did receive substantial support on the first ballot at the Democrats' nominating convention in New York in July, just two months after he survived the Republicans' effort to remove him from office.

In a letter to a friend one month later, Johnson showed impressive grace. That he called Lincoln the greatest American who ever lived is not shocking—he always praised his political benefactor. But he also forgave some of his enemies, notably Benjamin Butler. Though Johnson had harsh words for the man who led the charge to remove him, he said Butler's impressive military service for the Union mitigated his sins. Johnson's magnanimousness had limits. "I shall go to my grave with the firm belief that [Jefferson] Davis . . . should have been tried, convicted, and hanged for treason."[26] A few months later, he pardoned Davis and other Confederate leaders. Johnson was an elusive character to the end.

He left the White House quietly, but never tired of trying to return to public life. After several electoral defeats in Tennessee, in 1875 he was elected United States senator from the Volunteer State. He became colleagues with 13 of the men who had voted to convict him seven years earlier. Three months after he was sworn in for his new job, Johnson suffered a stroke and passed away the following day.

Most historians regard the Johnson impeachment as a partisan witch-hunt, but the reality is more complex. The further the event recedes in time, the more it becomes divorced from its historical context. If viewed solely as a question of whether Johnson's defiance of the Tenure of Office Act constituted an impeachable offense, the case is a slam dunk in Johnson's favor. But viewing the case that way would be like seeing the *Dred Scott* decision as turning on a technical question of jurisdiction, or *Brown v. Board of Education* as turning on the quality of the facilities in segregated schools. In other words, it ignores the history of racial oppression.

Out of context, Andrew Johnson's alleged wrongdoing seems technical and the impeachment episode simply a political tug-of-war. But that wasn't how the anti-Johnson forces viewed it. Consider these excerpts from Senator Sumner's opinion favoring Johnson's conviction: "This is one of the last great battles with slavery. . . . [D]riven from the field of war, this monstrous power has found a refuge in the Executive Mansion."[27] Sumner referred to Johnson as "the patron of rebels," and claimed that his refusal to break from slavery was "the transcendent crime of Andrew Johnson."[28]

These characterizations may have been hyperbolic, but Johnson provided fodder for them. He said in one speech that if blacks and whites could not get along, blacks would have to be colonized; he openly flirted with white supremacy and refused to criticize publicly the Black Codes that legally enforced an apartheid regime.

Imagine, as a thought experiment, if the House's articles of impeachment tracked Sumner's critique rather than relying on Johnson's discharge of Stanton. Suppose the House lumped together his many acts of opposition to Reconstruction into the following charge: "Through his obstruction of efforts to eliminate the vestiges of slavery, including measures providing blacks equal protection of the laws and the right of suffrage, the president has abetted a moral atrocity and thwarted the purpose for which 360,000 Union soldiers and President Lincoln gave their lives. He has thus demonstrated his unfitness for office at this crucial historical moment."

Though the outcome would likely have been the same, such an article would probably be looked on with more favor today than the articles actually adopted by the House. When we focus on Johnson's refusal to abolish the remnants of white racial domination and enslavement of black people, we can understand why his opponents felt compelled to remove him. They felt especially justified because Johnson was not elected into the Oval Office. On the great moral issue of the day, progress was blocked and evil enabled by an *accidental president*. Johnson's removal would not have undone the will of the people expressed at the ballot box. Indeed, it would have removed someone who arguably threatened the legacy of the man the American people had put in the White House.

To be fair, Johnson's views of Reconstruction were similar to Lincoln's, and the Radical Republicans had once toyed with the idea of impeaching Lincoln. Still, to say Republicans used impeachment as a political tool is to oversimplify. Slavery was not a routine political issue akin to fights over health care or taxes. Such issues, while important, lack the nation-defining moral clarity of racial justice, particularly in the immediate aftermath of the Civil War. Andrew Johnson's supporters insisted that he was not anti-black but rather favored a path to progress that was less punitive toward the South. But Republicans judged in good faith, and correctly, that Johnson was on the wrong side of history and morality.

It does not follow that Johnson's impeachment adhered to the letter and spirit of the Constitution. It did not, for reasons we will discuss in more detail in chapter six. For present purposes, a few things deserve mention. First, Andrew Johnson's term as president was winding down. Had Congress avoided the last resort of impeachment, he would have finished his term and stepped aside or else faced the voters. That much we know. It is an educated guess that had Johnson been convicted and removed, impeachment would have been resorted to far more readily thereafter—in the short term as revenge by Democrats, in the long term because of the historical precedent.

Even the failed effort to remove Johnson may have been costly. Many historians claim that it is no coincidence that few people today can name the half-dozen presidents to follow Andrew Johnson, believing that Johnson's impeachment and near-conviction weakened the presidency.

Perhaps the final word should be left to a Republican who resisted his party's push to remove the opposition president. Senator Lyman Trumbull, an Illinois Republican, close friend of Lincoln, and coauthor of the 13th

Amendment, was one of the seven Republicans who voted to acquit Johnson. Trumbull explained that if Johnson were convicted, "no future president will be safe who happens to differ with a majority of the House and two-thirds of the Senate on any measure deemed by them important. . . . And what then becomes of the checks and balances of the Constitution, so carefully devised and so vital?"[29]

THREE

DOWN GOES NIXON

It is tempting to say that Andrew Johnson's impeachment stemmed from his political vulnerability whereas Richard Nixon's imminent impeachment—averted only by his resignation—occurred because of his political strength. On this reading, the hubris caused by Nixon's 49-state landslide reelection in 1972 led him to regard himself as above the law and to abuse the prerogatives of his office. That view, however, neglects a crucial fact: The incident that set in motion the chain of events leading to Nixon's downfall occurred six months *before* the 1972 election, and reflected his campaign's sense of insecurity rather than invulnerability.

On June 17, 1972, District of Columbia police caught five men who had broken into the Democratic National Committee headquarters at the Watergate Hotel. The men, who wore surgical gloves and carried walkie-talkies and photographic equipment, apparently planned to bug the offices. Nixon's response to that failed intrusion, more than any other malfeasance, triggered his resignation two years later.

President Richard M. Nixon

On June 19, two days after the break-in, a pair of young *Washington Post* reporters broke the news that the burglars included former CIA agent James McCord, who served as security consultant to the Committee to Reelect the President ("CREEP"). Before long, it became clear that some of Nixon's aides actively and illegally sought to cover up the campaign's role in the break-in. A central question became whether the cover-up involved the nation's 37th president himself.

Nixon's press secretary, Ron Ziegler, downplayed the Watergate break-in as a "third-rate burglary." If Ziegler had been referring to the ineffectiveness of the operation, he would have had a point: The burglars botched the job. But his efforts to trivialize the break-in amounted to futile spin. A felonious burglary designed to perpetrate covert surveillance of an adversary political party is serious business. McCord and his fellow burglars were convicted of numerous criminal charges.

Far more serious, though, was the cover-up, if only because it ended up implicating the president. But despite the fact that Democrats controlled both houses of Congress, there was reluctance to pursue impeachment even as evidence of the cover-up emerged. This stemmed in part from the absence of precedent. Only 13 impeachment cases in United States history had reached a verdict in the Senate—mostly judges, along with one United States senator, one cabinet official, and President Andrew Johnson—yielding only four convictions, all of judges. Most of these cases involved corruption or drunkenness, circumstances bearing no similarity to the Watergate crimes. Moreover, the most recent impeachment had been in 1936, nearly four decades earlier. For all these reasons, these precedents were almost irrelevant.

The single example of a presidential impeachment counseled caution. Most historians and political scientists considered the impeachment of Andrew Johnson an unseemly, politically-motivated spectacle. That helps explain why no presidents thereafter were impeached, notwithstanding actions (such as the Teapot Dome Scandal during the Harding administration) that, under different circumstances, might have inspired loud calls for impeachment.

Thus, the Andrew Johnson ordeal could be seen as a case study counseling against impeachment. However, this century-old precedent provided limited guidance. Johnson was almost convicted, and senators who voted to acquit might have done so for any number of reasons. They may have believed that Johnson did nothing wrong, as he acted on a correct interpretation of the Tenure of Office Act and/or its unconstitutionality. Alternatively, they may have felt that he acted improperly but that the error did not rise to the level of a high crime or misdemeanor. Or they may have believed that he committed an impeachable offense but concluded that it was unnecessary and unwise to remove him when his term would expire shortly. The Johnson impeachment presented only a single, long-ago case that yielded no clear, agreed-upon narrative.*

---

* Thus, for example, historian David Stewart, author of a fine book about the Johnson impeachment, draws the opposite conclusion from the conventional wisdom that the Johnson case discredited

The House did not set in motion an impeachment process against Nixon until February 1974, by which time extensive evidence had already been gathered from three independent investigations: 1) the trial of the Watergate burglars before Judge John Sirica in federal court in the District of Columbia, as well as grand jury investigations flowing from that trial; 2) the Senate's Watergate Committee (more formally the "Select Committee on Presidential Campaign Activities"), chaired by folksy North Carolina Democrat Sam Ervin; and 3) the office of Special Prosecutor Archibald Cox and his successor, Leon Jaworski. In addition, reporting in several newspapers, especiallyby the *Washington Post's* Bob Woodward and Carl Bernstein, provided information used by the various investigators.

The evidence of White House wrongdoing uncovered by these investigations included some that predated

---

impeachment: "By coming so close to a conviction, the impeachers established that . . . the nation need not wait until the end of a four-year term to jettison a president." Moreover, "the experience chastened the most powerful person in the nation, who had committed many blunders, whether or not they warranted his removal from office." Finally, the peaceful impeachment process served as "a constitutional outlet for violent political passions." But Stewart does not address whether things would have turned violent had Johnson been convicted and removed. It is questionable to praise the pursuit of a remedy as a peaceful outlet if the peacefulness depends on failure. David Stewart, *Impeached: the Trial of Andrew Johnson and the Fight for Lincoln's Legacy* (New York: Simon & Schuster, 2009), p. 323.

the break-in at the Watergate Hotel. Most notably, back in September of 1971, the White House "plumbers" unit—so-called because of their mission to plug leaks in the administration—burglarized the office of a psychiatrist, Dr. Lewis Fielding, looking for material to discredit his patient, Daniel Ellsberg, the former defense analyst who leaked the *Pentagon Papers*. (The bungled break-in, and other government misconduct, led to dismissal of criminal charges against Ellsberg.)

Fairly early discoveries related to Watergate included the involvement of White House operatives Gordon Liddy and E. Howard Hunt in planning the break-in; the fact that CREEP, run by Nixon's former attorney general John Mitchell, controlled a secret fund (obtained in violation of campaign finance laws) that financed intelligence gathering and covert operations against Democrats; and the involvement in the Watergate cover-up of Nixon's top White House staffers, H.R. Haldeman and John Ehrlichman, and White House counsel John Dean, all of whom resigned as a result on April 30, 1973. In accepting their resignations, Nixon called Haldeman and Ehrlichman "two of the finest public servants it has been my privilege to know."[1] He said nothing about Dean, who was allegedly cooperating with prosecutors.

That trio of resignations accelerated inquiries into President Nixon's possible involvement in the cover-up. On May 1, the Senate by voice vote (albeit with only five senators present) asked Nixon to appoint a special prosecutor to investigate Watergate. On May 18, attorney general-designate Eliot Richardson appointed as special prosecutor Archibald Cox, a Harvard Law School professor and former solicitor general during the Kennedy and Johnson administrations.

One day earlier, Sam Ervin's Senate Select Committee, which had been established by vote of 77–0 in February, began holding hearings, televised on a rotating basis by ABC, CBS, and NBC until near the end of September. Public hearings continued through mid-November, the last few weeks covered only by public television. In all, the committee held 53 days of public hearings and heard testimony from 63 witnesses.

None was more important than John Dean, who testified under a grant of immunity from the committee after resigning from his White House position seven weeks earlier. (He could still could have been—and was—prosecuted in court; the immunity meant that his testimony before the committee could not be used against him at his trial.) For five days beginning June 25, 1973, Dean gave explosive testimony that propelled the investigation. The first day consisted of Dean reading a 246-page statement, prepared at the request of his attorneys, which outlined everything he knew pertaining to the Watergate break-in, the cover-up, and other wrongdoings involving the White House. The next four days, he relied on his prodigious memory in responding to questioning from the committee.

Dean claimed that the White House pressured the Watergate burglars to plead guilty and remain silent and that Nixon personally authorized "hush money" for that purpose. He asserted that he and Nixon discussed the Watergate cover-up on at least 35 occasions, going back to September 15, 1972, just a few months after the break-in (and not coincidentally the day a grand jury indicted the seven men responsible) and long before Nixon acknowledged even knowing there was a cover-up. Nixon actively participated in those discussions. He repeatedly counseled his underlings to "stonewall" investigators and essentially claim amnesia before a grand jury.

Dean also submitted to the committee a memorandum he authored and distributed to White House staff back in August 1971, stating the unofficial White House policy to explore "how we can use the available federal machinery to screw our political enemies."[2] Closely related, he disclosed that the White House urged the Internal Revenue Service (IRS) to conduct punitive tax audits against people on a long "enemies list" compiled by the White House.

Dean would be a particularly difficult witness to discredit, because he readily confessed to his own extensive involvement in illegal activities. Even so, Nixon's categorical denial of most of Dean's accusations created a potentially unresolvable he said/he said (not helped by Nixon's refusal to appear before the committee). That changed dramatically, however, on July 16, just a few weeks after Dean's testimony.

Herbert Kalmbach, formerly Nixon's personal attorney, testified that Dean and John Ehrlichman appealed to him to raise money for the Watergate defendants and their families. Kalmbach explained that he raised $220,000—money he came to realize was designed to buy the defendants' silence—and gave it to Anthony Ulasewicz, an "investigator" with White House connections, to deliver. (A few days later, Ulasewicz told the committee how he distributed large sums of cash in paper bags that he dropped off in lockers and telephone booths.)

Incredibly, Kalbmach's testimony, which corroborated Dean's and confirmed a criminal cover-up at the highest levels, barely made the news. It was overshadowed by testimony the same day from Alexander Butterfield, a retired air force officer who served as Nixon's appointments secretary from 1969 to 1973 before becoming administrator of the Federal Aviation Administration. Butterfield informed the Ervin Committee about taping devices that, in the spring of 1971, Nixon had installed in several rooms: the Oval Office, his office in the Executive Office Building, and the White House's cabinet room. These devices presumably recorded many of the president's conversations.

The superstitious may note that Butterfield first revealed the taping system in a private meeting with committee staff a few days earlier—on Friday, July 13. Dean had testified that he suspected conversations in the White House were recorded. Now a staff member asked Butterfield if there was any basis for Dean's suspicions. Butterfield replied, "I was hoping you fellows wouldn't ask me that,"[3] before making the stunning revelation.

Watergate special prosecutor Archibald Cox at a press conference, June 4, 1973. PHOTOGRAPH BY WARREN K. LEFFLER.

Immediately following Butterfield's public testimony, the Ervin Committee and Special Prosecutor Cox requested select tapes, but Nixon declined to provide them, claiming executive privilege. Both Cox and the committee then subpoenaed the tapes, and Judge Sirica ordered Nixon to comply with Cox's subpoena, a decision upheld by the U.S. Court of Appeals for the D.C. Circuit on October 12. Nixon still refused to comply, but proposed that Senator John Stennis, a Democrat from Mississippi and ally of the administration (not to mention notoriously hard of hearing), review and summarize the audio recordings for the special prosecutor's office. He also demanded that Cox thereafter cease seeking more tapes. Cox naturally declined the "compromise" offer that would have forfeited his victory in court.

On October 20, Nixon ordered Attorney General Richardson to fire Cox. (Under an agreement between the White House and Senate, only the Justice Department had that authority.) Richardson refused and resigned, as did Deputy Attorney General William Ruckelshaus. Solicitor General Robert Bork, next in line at the Justice Department, gave Cox the bad news. At a press conference that evening, Ron Ziegler also announced Nixon's intention to abolish the special prosecutor's office entirely and return the Watergate investigation to the Justice Department.

Hundreds of thousands of phone calls and telegrams bombarded Washington in protest of the so-called Saturday Night Massacre, but few public officials called for Nixon's resignation, in part because the vice presidency was at that moment vacant. Less than two weeks earlier, for reasons unrelated to Watergate, instead stemming primarily from misconduct in his days as governor of

Watergate landmark sign in Arlington, Virginia.

Maryland, Vice President Spiro Agnew had resigned. The person next in line of succession to the presidency, Speaker of the House Carl Albert, was a Democrat, and Nixon would not have considered resigning under the circumstances. Nor would Republicans have wanted him to.

Still, the Saturday Night Massacre seemed like a potential game-changer. To be sure, mention of impeachment had been bandied about six months earlier, following the April 30 resignations of Haldeman, Ehrlichman, and Dean, and an impeachment resolution had been introduced on July 31 by Father Robert Drinan, a Jesuit priest and leftist House member from Massachusetts. However, the resolution was largely ignored. After the firing of Cox, calls for impeachment became more frequent and were taken more seriously.

In the *New Yorker*, Elizabeth Drew quoted an anonymous Democratic House member as saying that the Saturday Night Massacre let "the genie out of the bottle. . . . What the President did over the weekend may not have been a high crime or misdemeanor, but it opened things up."[4] Indeed, within days of the Saturday Night Massacre, 57 senators introduced bills to establish a new special prosecutor. Nixon quickly backed down on his threat to abolish the office and announced that he would appoint a new special prosecutor to replace Cox.

On November 1, Acting Attorney General Bork appointed Leon Jaworski, a prominent Texas attorney who had been a prosecutor in the Nuremberg war trials, to succeed Cox.

Just two days earlier, on October 30, the House Judiciary Committee, consisting of 21 Democrats and 17 Republicans and chaired by New Jersey Democrat Peter Rodino, established an "impeachment inquiry" staff. The staff eventually included 43 lawyers, two of whom would later achieve political prominence: future Massachusetts governor William Weld and a recent Yale Law School graduate named Hillary Rodham. One of the congressmen on the committee, Iowa Democrat Ed Mezvinsky, would become father-in-law to Rodham's daughter, Chelsea Clinton, 37 years later.

Nixon did turn over some of the subpoenaed tapes ordered by Sirica and affirmed by the Court of Appeals, but two conversations that seemed particularly important (one with John Mitchell three days after the break-in and one with John Dean that Dean testified was damning) were missing. This prompted more calls for impeachment. In early November, Edward Brooke of Massachusetts became the first Republican senator to call on Nixon to resign.

Nixon steadfastly refused such invitations, and at a press conference on November 17 made one of the more memorable utterances of the entire Watergate affair. "People have got to know whether or not their president is a crook. Well, I am not a crook."[5]

Four days later, it was reported that one of the tapes the White House had turned over, involving a discussion between Nixon and Haldeman a few days after the break-in, contained 18.5 minutes in which nothing was audible. On November 26, Nixon's secretary, Rose Mary Woods, explained the gap in testimony before Judge Sirica. She claimed that she inadvertently recorded over the Nixon-Haldeman conversation in the course of transcribing it. As her alleged blunder would have required a contorted body position (in which she stepped on the recorder's foot pedal while reaching for the phone and somehow maintained that awkward position for a prolonged period), it became known as "the Rose Mary Stretch."

The next day, the Senate confirmed Gerald Ford as vice president by a vote of 92–3, and 10 days later the House did so by a vote of 387–35, removing a major impediment to Nixon's impeachment.*

As if Nixon didn't have enough problems, his private financial situation attracted scrutiny during this period.

---

* In a quirky footnote to history, one of the three "no" votes in the Senate came from Missouri senator Thomas Eagleton, briefly the Democrats' vice presidential nominee the previous year, until he was forced to step down after revelations that he had been hospitalized for depression on several occasions.

House Judiciary Subcommittee questioning President Gerald Ford on pardoning former President Richard Nixon, October 17, 1974.
PHOTOGRAPH BY THOMAS J. O'HALLORAN.

It was revealed that he claimed a $570,000 income tax deduction for donating his vice presidential papers to the government and that the government paid for improvements on his private homes in Florida and California. Under pressure from public interest groups, on December 8 Nixon released his tax returns for 1969–72. They showed that he paid a combined total of $6,000 in income tax for 1970–72. (Though he often emphasized his humble beginnings and refusal to capitalize on his public service, Nixon had in fact become a millionaire by this time.) Months later, the IRS determined that he owed $476,000 in back taxes and interest.

Meanwhile, on January 15, 1974, a six-member panel of electronics experts jointly selected by the White House and Special Prosecutor Jaworski's office to study the missing 18.5 minutes of Haldeman-Nixon conversation reported its findings to Judge Sirica. The group unanimously concluded that the gap on the tape was caused by at least five deliberate erasures, debunking the "Rose Mary Woods Stretch" explanation.

On January 30, in his State of the Union address, President Nixon vowed to cooperate with the House impeachment inquiry "in any way I consider consistent with my responsibility to the office of the presidency," while reiterating that he would withhold requested materials whose release would compromise the need for confidentiality in high-level conversations. He urged a speedy resolution of the investigation, remarking that "one year of Watergate is enough." The next day Sam Ervin retorted that "one minute of Watergate was too much" and placed the blame for the delay on Nixon's failure to cooperate.[6]

On February 6, by a vote of 410–4, the House formally authorized the Judiciary Committee to investigate the propriety of impeaching Nixon and empowered the committee to draft articles of impeachment if appropriate. It also gave the committee subpoena power.

Just two weeks later, the impeachment inquiry staff weighed in on the ongoing debate over the purpose and scope of impeachment, drafting a memorandum arguing that impeachment does not require criminal behavior but rather any conduct that involves "undermining the integrity of office, disregard of constitutional duties and oath of office, arrogation of power, abuse of the governmental process."[7] However, the memorandum acknowledged that impeachment is a grave step reserved for cases of serious misconduct that violate constitutional norms and duties.

On February 28, Nixon's legal team, led by Boston attorney James St. Clair, submitted a written response to the committee. (This wasn't St. Clair's first brush with history. At the Joseph McCarthy hearings in 1954, he assisted Joseph Welch, who famously asked Senator McCarthy, "Have you no shame?") He argued, as Nixon's defenders would throughout the process, that an overly broad view of impeachment would destroy the fundamental principle of separation of powers. St. Clair insisted that a president could not be impeached unless he committed an indictable crime such as treason or bribery. At a press conference three days earlier, Nixon himself maintained that only a criminal offense justifies impeachment.

On March 1, the Watergate grand jury indicted Haldeman, Ehrlichman, and Mitchell for obstruction of justice related to the cover-up of the Watergate break-in. They also handed down indictments of Mitchell and Haldeman for perjury before the Ervin Committee and Mitchell and Ehrlichman for perjury before the grand jury itself.

Five days later, St. Clair announced that Nixon would cooperate fully with requests from the House

Judiciary Committee for specific tapes and documents. He would also answer written questions from the committee and even sit down for interviews with members of the committee.

The next day, March 7, brought more bad news for the president's (former) men: Ehrlichman, Charles Colson, and G. Gordon Liddy were indicted for their role in the burglary of the office of Dr. Lewis Fielding, Daniel Ellsberg's psychiatrist, back in 1971.

On March 8, just two days after announcing Nixon's plans for far-reaching cooperation with the Judiciary Committee, St. Clair declared a change of course: Nixon would turn over only materials he considered directly related to the Watergate break-in and cover-up, and planned to withhold some of the tapes and documents the committee had requested.

On April 4, Chairman Rodino opened a session of the Judiciary Committee by reading a statement concerning the White House's noncompliance with requests for tapes and documents: "The patience of this committee is now wearing thin. . . . We can subpoena them if we must."[8] When the only response was a letter by St. Clair saying that a review of the requested material was under way and might take weeks to complete, the committee made good on its threat. On April 11, by a vote of 33–3, it subpoenaed 42 tapes of conversations involving Nixon. (One of the three "no" votes came from a 32-year-old Mississippi Republican, Trent Lott, who would become Senate minority leader decades later and thus a leading figure at the impeachment trial of Bill Clinton.)

One week later, another subpoena was served on Nixon, this one initiated by Special Prosecutor Jaworski and signed by Judge Sirica. It ordered President Nixon to turn over memoranda and tapes covering 64 conversations deemed potentially relevant to the forthcoming criminal tri-

Nixon operative, G. Gordon Liddy

als of Haldeman, Ehrlichman, Mitchell, and four other defendants charged with Watergate-related crimes.

In a nationally televised address on April 29, Nixon pledged to give the House Judiciary Committee edited transcripts of the conversations in question, but warned that impeachment "would put the nation through a wrenching ordeal." He remarked, apropos the 18.5-minute gap in a key tape, "How it was caused is still a mystery to me."[9]

The next day the White House made public more than 1,200 pages of edited transcripts of the president's conversations. (The editing included countless insertions of "Expletive Deleted.") However, Nixon refused to turn over the actual tapes or to comply with the special prosecutor's subpoena.

The transcripts included substantial damning material. On the day the Watergate burglars were indicted, Nixon praised John Dean for "very skilful[ly] putting your fingers in the leaks that have sprung here and sprung there," which certainly sounded like reference to maintaining a cover-up. In another conversation, Dean said that buying the silence of the defendants would require one million dollars. Nixon replied, "We could get that. . . . You could get a million dollars. You could get it in cash. I know where it could be gotten." And he later said about such a payoff, "It would seem to me that would be worthwhile." In a different conversation, Nixon instructed Assistant Attorney General Henry Petersen, who was at the time investigating Watergate as head of the Justice Department's criminal division, "You have got to maintain the presidency out of this."

On May 1, Chairman Rodino sent a one-sentence letter to the president on behalf of the House Judiciary Committee advising him that he had failed to comply with the Committee's subpoena of April 11. The following day Nixon responded that any further disclosures of White House conversations would be contrary to the public interest.

On May 7, St. Clair announced that no tapes or transcripts would be given to the special prosecutor and nothing additional to the House Judiciary Committee. Two days later, the committee began official impeachment hearings. As in all its prior work, the committee aimed for bipartisanship. The majority and minority had formed a single staff jointly appointed, and held most deliberations in private to reduce partisan pressures. Still, divisions emerged. In their sessions behind closed doors, Chairman Rodino and the committee's chief counsel, John Doar, presented a pattern of misconduct and Democratic members voiced support for impeachment, but most Republicans held out. They echoed the White House view that only indictable offenses were impeachable and demanded greater specificity in the evidence against Nixon before presidential impeachment could be seriously contemplated.

In late July, the committee televised hearings—roughly 80 hours spanning six days. A recurring question during the hearings was one famously posed by Republican Senator Howard Baker during the hearings of the Ervin Committee (of which Baker was vice chairman): "What did the President know and when did he know it?" The more material that came out with respect to that question, and other White House improprieties, the more the sentiment swung toward impeachment, although during the summer there remained sharp partisan division in both Congress and the country at large.

On May 20, Judge Sirica issued a formal order requiring Nixon to turn over the tapes of the 64 conversations requested by Special Prosecutor Jaworski. The White House announced that it would defy the order and appeal all the way to the Supreme Court. The same day, *Newsweek* quoted Senator Barry Goldwater, the Republican presidential nominee in 1964, saying that the time had come for Nixon to think about stepping down.

Later in the month, the House Judiciary Committee sent the White House a strongly worded letter stating that it would have to consider whether the refusal to turn over materials might itself constitute a ground for impeachment. The vote to send the letter was 28–10, with eight Republicans going along. On June 6, the *Los Angeles Times* reported that back in March the federal grand jury that indicted Haldeman, Ehrlichman and others for their involvement in the Watergate cover-up had named Nixon as an unindicted co-conspirator.

On June 24, Charles Colson pleaded guilty and received the stiffest sentence to date for any of the Watergate defendants, one to three years in prison plus a $5000 fine, for obstruction of justice based on efforts to defame Daniel Ellsberg and influence the jury prior to Ellsberg's trial. In a statement in the courtroom, Colson pointed a finger at the president, who, he said, "on numerous occasions urged me to disseminate damaging information about Ellsberg."[10]

On June 27, the Ervin Committee released its 1,094-page report detailing the findings from its year-long investigation. The report made no explicit recommendations, but reasonable readers would see it as supporting Nixon's impeachment, as Chairman Ervin all but admitted to a reporter: "You can draw the picture of a horse in two ways. You can draw a very good likeness of a horse, and say nothing. Or you can draw a picture of a horse, and write under it: 'This is a horse.' We just drew the picture."[11]

The next day, St. Clair made his first appearance

before the House Judiciary Committee, and maintained that Nixon did not learn about the Watergate cover-up until March of 1973 and never approved the payment of hush money to the defendants.

On July 8, in a special summer session to expedite the matter, the Supreme Court heard argument in *U.S. v. Nixon* revolving around the president's refusal to turn over the tapes subpoenaed by Special Prosecutor Jaworski. Nixon's lawyers argued, among other things, that the president gets to determine the scope of executive privilege and the Court should not intervene in this intramural dispute within the executive branch between the president and the special prosecutor. Jaworski countered that the courts must decide this issue, lest the president trot out executive privilege to shield criminal behavior by himself or his subordinates.

Four days later, John Ehrlichman, G. Gordon Liddy, and two other former White House aides were convicted of conspiracy for their role in the break-in at the office of Daniel Ellsberg's psychiatrist back in 1971.

On July 19, the House Judiciary Committee, having heard testimony from dozens of witnesses and reviewed hundreds of documents, heard the case for impeachment summarized by its lead counsel, John Doar. (As deputy assistant attorney general and later assistant attorney general of the Civil Rights Division under Presidents Kennedy and Johnson, Doar had already made his mark in history.) Doar recommended in no uncertain terms the impeachment of Nixon, citing his "enormous crimes."[12]

Nixon's press secretary, Ron Ziegler, who had earlier dismissed the Watergate break-in as a "third-rate burglary," now dismissed Doar as a "partisan ideologue" operating in a "kangaroo court."[13]

July 24 brought the most decisive event in the two-year saga. In an opinion signed by Chief Justice Warren Burger, a Nixon appointee, the Supreme Court unanimously rejected Nixon's claim of executive privilege and ruled that the White House must turn over the subpoenaed tapes. The White House announced that it would comply.

That evening, at 7:45 p.m., the House Judiciary Committee began debate over impeachment, with each of its 38 members allotted 15 minutes. After roughly one hour, and four speakers, Chairman Rodino cryptically announced that he was "compelled to recess" the hearing for an unspecified period of time. It would later be learned that an anonymous bomb threat had been phoned in. Capitol police and bomb-sniffing dogs swept the hearing room and found nothing. Forty minutes later, the hearing resumed and remained in session until almost 11:00 p.m.

In the many hours of statements that night and over the next few days, perhaps the most memorable moment came when Barbara Jordan, an African American congresswoman from Texas, struck a personal note. She observed that when the Constitution was completed, "I was not included in that We the People. I felt somehow for many years that George Washington and Alexander

Hamilton left me out by mistake. But through the process of amendment, interpretation, and court decision I have finally been included in We the People."[14]

The Preamble to the Constitution declares the goal of a "more perfect union." The union became "more perfect" when it embraced all Americans, and more perfect still when Congress opened its doors to people like Barbara Jordan. Now the gifted orator explained why that unachievable quest for perfection required removing a president who dishonored that very Constitution. "I am not going to sit here and be an idle spectator to the diminution, the subversion, the destruction" of the nation's founding and foundational document.

On July 27, the Judiciary Committee passed an article of impeachment alleging obstruction of justice. On July 29, the committee passed a second article accusing President Nixon of abuse of power, and on July 30 a third based on the administration's defiance of the committee's subpoenas to turn over tapes and other documents. The committee sent a report to the full House of Representatives recommending impeachment on these three grounds.

The committee rejected two proposed articles of impeachment. One was based on tax fraud and receipt of unconstitutional emoluments (stemming from government expenditures on Nixon's private homes), and the other was based on the secret bombing of Cambodia in 1969 and 1970—more than 3000 raids that the administration concealed and lied about.

Article 1, the obstruction of justice charge revolving around the Watergate cover-up, laid out nine specific acts of wrongdoing, including approving hush money and promising favorable treatment to various potential witnesses; making and encouraging others to make false statements to law enforcement; and more generally "interfering with the conduct of investigations" by the Department of Justice of the United States, the Federal Bureau of Investigation (FBI), the special prosecutor, and congressional committees. Article 1 passed the Committee by a 27–11 vote.

Article 2, the abuse of power charge, included several subsections alleging misuse of the IRS to harass political enemies and misuse of the FBI and other government bodies to conduct illegal surveillance of political enemies. It passed 28–10.

Article 3, concerning Nixon's failure to comply with subpoenas to produce evidence, passed 21–17.

The committee rejected the articles based on income tax invasion and receipt of emoluments and the secret bombing of Cambodia by votes of 26–12.

The full House never voted on impeachment. On August 5, the White House turned over the Court-ordered tapes, which laid bare Nixon's involvement in the cover-up, including his effort to have the Central Intelligence Agency (CIA) stop the FBI's investigation into the Watergate break-in. His support in Congress and in the nation evaporated. All 10 members of the House Judiciary Committee who had voted against the articles of impeachment declared that they would now support at least Article 1.

On August 7, a delegation of Republican leaders, including former presidential nominee Senator Barry Goldwater, paid a visit to Nixon and urged him to resign. The next day, he did.

Even if he had been convicted by the Senate rather than resigned, Nixon would have remained in legal jeopardy. As noted in chapter one, a president removed from office may still be prosecuted for crimes in the court system. However, Nixon could breathe easier one month later. On September 8, his presidential successor, Gerald Ford, granted Nixon a "full, free, and absolute pardon" for any offenses he committed while president.

The Nixon saga vindicated the founding fathers' vision of impeachment. The process was by no means entirely apolitical: The majority of the Judiciary Committee voted along party lines. But the result was exactly what we would hope for: Republicans' resistance to impeachment ensured that it did not happen too easily or prematurely. To the contrary, more than two years elapsed between the initial evidence of wrongdoing and Nixon's resignation. Eventually, enough Republicans came around to produce the peaceful removal of an unfit president. As a body, the House Judiciary Committee ably differentiated among the various charges and correctly identified which ones warranted impeachment.

The committee probably voted correctly with respect to at least four of the five proposed articles of impeachment. Little doubt remains about the first two. Nixon's guilt with respect to the obstruction of justice and abuse of power charges has become ever more apparent over the years with the release of more taped conversations and other evidence. He clearly participated in the Watergate cover-up and misused various executive branch agencies in an effort to harm his political enemies. Few observers dispute that such misconduct was sufficiently serious to warrant impeachment.

A case can be made that the third article, based on Nixon's noncompliance with the committee's subpoenas, was premature, that as with Andrew Johnson's response to the Tenure of Office Act, Nixon was entitled to withhold materials until courts determined that he had no basis for doing so. His defiance, while perhaps revealing and certainly maddening to members of the committee, arguably did not rise to the level of an impeachable offense. (On the other hand, the withholding of evidence made it difficult to get at the truth of the other accusations. Not impeaching on this charge might have established a perverse precedent for presidents facing scandal.) Significantly, this article squeaked by, receiving zero votes from Republicans and two "no" votes from Democrats.

The decision not to impeach based on Nixon's alleged tax fraud and wrongful receipt of emoluments made sense on constitutional grounds. These alleged improprieties were unrelated to his official duties as president. They could be prosecuted in criminal court after Nixon left office (or at least the tax fraud could) but were not a strong basis for impeachment.

With respect to the bombing of Cambodia, opponents of impeachment made several arguments that proved persuasive even to many Democrats: Some leading members of Congress knew about the bombing and acquiesced; even after the entire Congress knew, they did not move to stop the bombings for some time, thereby effectively ratifying the bombing campaign; earlier full disclosure to Congress conceivably could have jeopardized the mission and compromised national security; and the matter was subsequently resolved by passage of the War Powers Act, which clarified when and how presidents must consult Congress when undertaking military operations.

The merits aside, pragmatism dictated forgoing these charges. The three articles of impeachment that passed described a clear and serious misuse of presidential powers. To mix in the tax fraud and emoluments claims at the Senate trial would have diluted and even trivialized the articles of impeachment that dealt with meatier matters. In the criminal law, prosecutors routinely make tactical decisions about what to charge. Senators, whom we expect to be attuned to political realities, surely may do the same.

While a powerful case can be made that the secret bombing of Cambodia violated the Constitution, the use of U.S. military force abroad frequently occurs in gray areas. Every president since and including John F. Kennedy—and many before him—used military force in controversial operations not clearly authorized by the Constitution. These controversies are best resolved in the normal political process, with resort to the courts as necessary, and perhaps by constitutional amendment to clarify the branches' respective authority. Impeachment is not the proper venue for adjudicating such disputes.

Nevertheless, a reasonable case can be made that secret bombings of a noncombatant country were beyond the pale. But context always comes into play, and here the context included the existence of more cut-and-dried bases for impeachment. Had Nixon been impeached over the bombings, the Senate trial might have become a long and involved referendum on the Vietnam War, deflecting attention from his more obvious misdeeds and impeding the prospects of a bipartisan outcome.

One major difference between the cases of Andrew Johnson and Richard Nixon is that Johnson was never elected president, whereas Nixon received over 60 percent of the vote in a landslide of historic proportions. All things being equal, that would make the impeachment of Johnson more amenable. But the more salient difference cuts the other way—Nixon clearly committed impeachable offenses.

The overly tidy verdict of history renders the Johnson impeachment a partisan failure and the Nixon saga a bipartisan success. We are on safe ground in considering the Johnson case a failure and Nixon case a success in terms of outcome: Johnson should not have been impeached, whereas Nixon should have been (and would have been had he not resigned). However, with respect to partisanship, we should be careful not to oversimplify the differences between the cases.

When the House Judiciary Committee released its final report on August 20, 1974, two weeks after Nixon's resignation, all 38 members opined that impeachment would have been appropriate. The release of damning tapes on August 5 made converts of those Republicans who had voted against all the articles of impeachment. But if we look at the actual votes cast, the Johnson and Nixon cases were not too dissimilar in terms of partisanship. Seven senators voted across party lines to acquit Johnson—the exact number of House members who crossed party lines to vote to impeach Nixon. Indeed, for all the claims of bipartisanship, in the Nixon case just shy of half the members of the Judiciary Committee (18 out of 38) voted the party line on all five articles. Eight Democrats voted for all five proposed grounds of impeachment and 10 Republican senators voted against all five.

To be clear, bipartisanship played a decisive and wholly welcome role in both the Johnson and Nixon cases. In the case of Nixon, historians rightly emphasize the critical roles of Woodward and Bernstein, Mark Felt ("Deep Throat"), Judge John Sirica, and Special Prosecutors Cox and Jaworski in bringing out the truth. They also praise the work of Democrats Sam Ervin and Peter Rodino, who chaired the respective Senate and House committees that investigated Watergate. But the indispensable efforts of these people would not have sufficed to remove Nixon from office but for the courage and patriotism of some Republicans in Congress. Just as the so-called Seven Tall Men spared the nation a catastrophic outcome in the trial of Andrew Johnson, the seven Republicans who voted to impeach Richard Nixon merit a special place in the pantheon of Watergate heroes.

Highest honors are reserved for Maryland Representative Lawrence Hogan, the first Republican on the Judiciary Committee to announce his support for impeachment and the only Republican to vote yes on all three of the articles that passed. Hogan explained the basis of his vote as follows:

> The thing that's so appalling to me is that the President, when this whole idea was suggested to him, didn't, in righteous indignation, rise up and say, "Get out of here, you're in the office of the President of the United States. How can you talk about blackmail and bribery and keeping witnesses silent? This is the Presidency of the United States." But my President didn't do that.[15]

As was the case with the Republican senators who acquitted Johnson, Hogan's heroism proved costly. He ran for governor of Maryland that year but failed to get the Republican nomination. (His son was elected governor of Maryland some 40 years later.) Political observers attributed Hogan's defeat to his disloyalty to his party during the impeachment process.

Another Republican member of the Judiciary Committee to vote for impeachment, Virginia's Caldwell Butler, was a first-term congressman with a reputation for integrity who knew that he owed his place in Congress to Nixon—just two years earlier he had ridden the coattails of Nixon's landslide. In his statement during the final debate on July 25, Butler acknowledged his debt to Nixon but noted that Republicans had long complained about and campaigned against Democratic corruption. "Watergate is *our* shame. . . . If we fail to impeach, we will have condoned and left unpunished a course of conduct totally inconsistent with the reasonable expectations of the American people."[16] He, too, put patriotism above party.

William Cohen, a 33-year-old congressman from Maine, angered Republicans throughout the process. In May, when the Judiciary Committee voted to send a letter to Nixon complaining about his failure to comply with the committee's subpoenas, Cohen was the only Republican to vote in favor. In the floor debate over impeachment in July, he addressed the claim by some Republicans that every president engages in the kind of misconduct Nixon stood accused of. "Democracy may be eroded away by degree," Cohen said. "Its survival will be determined by the degree to which we will tolerate those silent and subtle subversions."[17] Cohen's career in public service, marked by his willingness to work across the aisle, culminated in his service as Secretary of Defense under a Democratic president, Bill Clinton.

Although the Nixon case never went to trial in the Senate, some Republican senators distinguished themselves along the way. Howard Baker and Lowell Weicker, members of the Ervin Committee, showed more interest in arriving at truth than in automatically backing the president from their party, thus infuriating Republicans nationwide who for a long time supported Nixon overwhelmingly. Kudos also to Barry Goldwater, who helped convince Nixon to resign and spare the nation the trauma of a drawn-out trial and active removal of the president. ("You can only be lied to so often," Goldwater allegedly told his fellow Republican senators, explaining his support for Nixon's departure.)[18] Ditto Elliot Richardson, a lifelong Republican whose refusal to fire Special Prosecutor Cox sent an important message about the rule of law and marked a decisive blow against Nixon.

If the Nixon ordeal reminded us of the value of bipartisanship, it also reinforced the idea that indictable crimes are not needed for impeachment. Much of the debate over Nixon's fate throughout 1973–74, both in the country at large and within the congressional investigative committees, revolved around that question. (Eventually it became clear that Nixon's conduct *did* include criminal behavior. Indeed, as noted, a grand jury named Nixon an unindicted co-conspirator.) It came to be widely accepted that non-criminal behavior can constitute an impeachable offense. The Constitution authorizes removing the president whose improper actions threaten our system and render that individual unfit, and actions may fit that description without involving crimes on the books.

FOUR

THE CLINTON PREDICAMENT

A little more than a century separated the end of the Andrew Johnson impeachment ordeal and the beginning of Richard Nixon's. After the latter, it would be merely two decades before the next serious impeachment effort was set in motion.

On August 9, 1994, almost 20 years to the day that Nixon resigned, a three-judge panel appointed former U.S. solicitor general Kenneth Starr as independent counsel to investigate the 42nd president of the United States, William Jefferson Clinton. Clinton's defenders would insist that the entire ordeal was about sex, but the subject of Starr's initial investigation was hardly sexy: Clinton's involvement as an investor in the Whitewater real estate development in Arkansas in the 1970s and early '80s, a decade before he was elected president. But when it comes to independent counsels, way leads on to way and investigations dramatically change course. Starr's inquiry eventually led to Clinton's impeachment on charges unrelated to Whitewater.

In May 1994, 15 months into Clinton's presidency,

an Arkansas government employee named Paula Jones filed suit against Clinton in federal court in Arkansas, demanding $700,000 in damages for sexually harassing her in May 1991 while he was governor of Arkansas. Ms. Jones alleged that, at a conference of state employees, Clinton had a state trooper tell Jones that he wanted to see her in his hotel room. The trooper escorted her to Clinton's suite, where Clinton exposed himself and asked Jones to kiss his genitals. When she refused his advances, he told her to keep quiet about the interaction.

As civil suits tend to do, *Jones v. Clinton* dragged on for some time with limited progress. The same could be said of Independent Counsel Starr's investigation of Whitewater. Starr was actually not the first independent counsel to probe Whitewater. In January 1994, Attorney General Janet Reno had appointed Robert Fiske to that post. On June 30, Fiske produced an interim report finding no wrongdoing by Clinton. On that same day, however, Clinton signed into law a bill replacing the old "special prosecutor" office with an "independent counsel." Whereas special prosecutors had been chosen by the attorney general, the new statute called for appointment of the independent counsel by a "Special Division"—a panel of three court of appeals judges themselves appointed by the chief justice.

Reno requested that Fiske be appointed to the new position in order to maintain continuity with his investigation. However, the panel, led by conservative Judge David Sentelle of the D.C. Circuit, opted for Starr instead. Although Fiske was a Republican, in no way beholden to Reno or President Clinton, the panel claimed that his earlier appointment by Reno created an appearance of impropriety. Starr himself was a long-time Republican and federal court of appeals judge before his selection as solicitor general by President George H.W. Bush. He was in private practice when tapped to be independent counsel.

Monica Lewinsky government identification photo, dated 1997

While Starr investigated Whitewater, President Clinton entered far more dangerous territory. In November 1995, he and Monica Lewinsky, a 22-year-old unpaid intern who worked in the West Wing of the White House, commenced an intimate relationship. Over the next six months, on at least eight occasions Clinton and Lewinsky engaged in sexual relations in rooms adjacent to the Oval Office. Their encounters typically involved oral sex but never intercourse.

In April 1996, Lewinsky was transferred to a secretarial job with the Defense Department, allegedly a deliberate move by White House aides to put distance between the president and his intern. Though Clinton allegedly broke off the relationship in May, he and Lewinsky remained in touch, occasionally exchanging gifts and engaging in phone sex. She sometimes visited the White House, where she was ushered in to see the president by his secretary, Betty Currie. Clinton and Lewinsky engaged in sexual relations twice more in early 1997, before Clinton again broke things off in May.

Thereafter, their relationship consisted largely of phone calls in which Lewinsky, who disliked her job at the Pentagon, beseeched the president to help her find work elsewhere. He put her in touch with his friend Vernon Jordan, a prominent Washington attorney whose intervention eventually helped Lewinsky land a job with Revlon, though the offer was later rescinded.

Meanwhile, on May 27, the Supreme Court ruled unanimously that Paula Jones's lawsuit against President Clinton could go forward while he was in office. Eight justices stated that conclusion uncategorically, whereas Stephen Breyer left the door open for the president to establish that the lawsuit would interfere with his constitutional responsibilities (in which case it would be postponed until he was no longer in office).

After the Supreme Court decision, the trial judge in the suit, Susan Webber Wright, ruled that during pretrial "discovery" (the legal process for obtaining information from the other side), Jones's lawyers could inquire about improper relationships between Clinton and other women who served under him. Accordingly, they sought to depose Lewinsky, whose relationship with Clinton they learned about from her friend Linda Tripp. Upon hearing from his attorneys that Lewinsky's name was on the list of people Jones's lawyers wished to depose, Clinton encouraged Lewinsky to claim that her visits to the White House were either to see Betty Currie or to deliver documents.

In December, Lewinsky received a subpoena to appear for a deposition in late January and to bring with her any gifts she had received from Clinton. Lewinsky drafted an affidavit, with the assistance of counsel, asserting that she had not had a sexual relationship with Clinton. She also transferred to Currie some of Clinton's gifts to her.

On January 17, 1998, Jones's lawyers deposed Clinton. He denied having had sexual relations with Lewinsky. The next day, he summoned Currie to his office and made highly suggestive comments that appeared to be telling Currie what to say if she were asked about his relationship with Lewinsky. ("We were never really alone" and "Monica came on to me and I never touched her, right?") A few days later, he had another conversation with Currie along the same lines.

On the day before Clinton's deposition, Independent Counsel Starr, now in his fourth year investigating Whitewater, obtained from the U.S. Court of Appeals for the District of Columbia permission to expand his investigation to include Clinton's possible obstruction of justice with respect to the Jones's lawsuit. Starr knew about Clinton's relationship with Lewinsky from Tripp, who secretly taped her conversations with Lewinsky about

Clinton. (Tripp claimed to do so to protect herself from perjury if she were deposed by Jones's lawyers, though circumstantial evidence suggests that she wished to bring Clinton down.)

On that same day, attorneys from Starr's office approached Lewinsky and told her she was vulnerable to prosecution for perjury and obstruction of justice. They offered her immunity if she would record conversations between herself and Clinton and Jordan. She declined.

When media reports revealed Starr's investigation of his involvement with Lewinsky, Clinton publicly denied any sexual relationship, most famously in his nationally televised declaration on January 26 that "I did not have sexual relations with that woman."

On April 1, Judge Wright granted summary judgment for Clinton in the Paula Jones lawsuit, finding that even if Clinton did what Jones accused him of, his conduct did not rise to the level of "criminal sexual assault" (as Jones had alleged) because it involved no physical contact, and she could not prevail on her claim of sexual harassment under Title VII of the Civil Rights Act because she failed to show that she suffered "tangible job detriment." Jones's lawyers announced their intention to appeal the decision.

With the lawsuit at least temporarily sidelined, Clinton's denials held up for several months. They began to unravel on July 28 when Lewinsky accepted an offer of immunity from Starr's office. She testified before a grand jury and turned over extensive documentation of

President Bill Clinton at his desk in the Oval Office

her affair with Clinton (which was buttressed by several witnesses, including Bettie Currie and secret service agents). The smoking gun, so to speak, was Lewinsky's blue dress, stained by semen shown by DNA tests to have come from Clinton.

Before the results of the DNA tests were announced, Clinton, from the White House, testified before a grand jury over closed-circuit television on August 17. He acknowledged "inappropriate intimate contact" with Lewinsky but, while refusing to go into detail, insisted that he had nevertheless not testified falsely during his deposition in the Jones case. Rather, Clinton claimed to have clung to the definition of "sexual relations" given at the deposition, which did not specifically include oral-genital contact. Thus, he maintained, his encounters with Lewinsky "did not constitute sexual relations as I understood the term to be defined at my January 17, 1998, deposition."

Clinton also insisted that he spoke truthfully when testifying at the deposition that he and Lewinsky were rarely alone, since there were other people "in the vicinity." He denied having encouraged her or Bettie Currie to lie or to conceal evidence in any way. He claimed that his instructions to Currie were designed solely to refresh her recollection.

On September 9, three weeks later, Independent Counsel Starr submitted a report to Congress. The Starr Report stated at the outset that it contained "substantial and credible information that President William Jefferson Clinton committed [multiple] acts that may constitute grounds for an impeachment,"[1] most of which stemmed from lying under oath during his deposition in the Jones case and before the grand jury; attempting to suborn Betty Currie; and attempting to obstruct justice by encouraging Lewinsky to file a false affidavit and not to comply with the subpoena to turn over gifts.*

Calls for Clinton's impeachment, which had become frequent once he acknowledged the sexual relationship

---

* The Starr Report mentioned the Whitewater land deal, which Starr was initially hired to investigate, only in passing. Robert Ray, who succeeded Starr as independent counsel when Starr stepped down in 1998, later concluded that there was insufficient evidence to proceed against Clinton with respect to Whitewater.

with Lewinsky a few weeks earlier, intensified. When on October 5 the House Judiciary Committee met to consider impeachment for the first time, battle lines were drawn. Republican members, who were in the majority, harkened back to the last time the House had considered impeachment—Watergate. Democrats scoffed at the comparison. Democrat John Conyers from Michigan, the one member of the Judiciary Committee who had sat on the committee in 1974, said, "This is not Watergate. It is an extramarital affair."[2] (Ironically, Conyers would be forced to resign in 2017 over allegations of sexual harassment.) South Carolina Republican Lindsey Graham was a rare member to stake out a middle ground: "Is this Watergate or *Peyton Place*? I don't know."[3]

But most members knew exactly how they felt, and the respective opening statements by majority and minority counsel suggested an unbridgeable divide. Republican counsel David Schippers described "an ongoing series of deliberate and direct assaults by Mr. Clinton upon the justice system of the United States,"[4] whereas Democratic counsel Abbe Lowell insisted that Clinton's wrongdoing came down to three words: "lying about sex."[5] The *serious* wrongdoing in the case, according to Lowell, was at Clinton's expense: He was the victim of a politically motivated lawsuit and an overzealous independent counsel.

The committee adopted by straight party line vote (21–16) a proposal by its chairman, Republican Henry Hyde of Illinois, modeled closely on a similar effort to investigate Watergate a quarter century earlier. The resolution, if adopted by the full House, would establish an "impeachment inquiry" by the committee and give it subpoena power.

Unlike in the Judiciary Committee, sentiments in the full House of Representatives did not break down *entirely* along partisan lines: A number of conservative Democrats pronounced themselves disgusted by Clinton's behavior and favored pursuing impeachment. When on October 8 the House authorized an inquiry into impeachment, the vote was 258–176, with 31 Democrats joining Republicans. (By contrast, the House vote to pursue impeachment of Nixon had been 410–4.)

In the midterm elections less than a month later, Democrats did surprisingly well, gaining five seats in the House. It was the first time since the early 19th century that the president's party did not lose seats (often dozens) in the sixth year of an administration. The elections seemed like a clear repudiation of the move to impeach Clinton, and left the Republicans with just a tiny majority—223 members to 211 Democrats. Speaker Newt Gingrich, who had pushed impeachment, resigned from the House.

If the election gave the Republicans second thoughts about impeachment, it did not stop them from moving forward. This may seem surprising, but in 1998 impeachment did not seem quite as big a deal as it once had. To some extent, it had been normalized by Watergate. Whereas the Andrew Johnson fiasco led to avoidance of impeachment for the next century, the successful pursuit of Richard Nixon produced the reverse effect. In the 25 years between the Nixon and Clinton impeachment efforts, there had been six serious impeachment investigations and three actual impeachments. (There had been none in the previous 38 years.) All three involved judges, and all three resulted in convictions in the Senate. The most recent two involved perjury—Alcee Hastings and Walter Nixon (no relation to Richard), convicted in 1988 and 1989 respectively. Hastings was elected to Congress in 1993, and thus voted on the Clinton impeachment!

Sixty-seven of the House members who voted on Clinton's impeachment were in Congress during the Nixon impeachment process, including seven who served on the House Judiciary Committee that approved articles of impeachment against Nixon. Seven members of the Senate who tried Clinton had been in Congress during the proceedings involving Nixon. Fred Thompson, a lawyer for the Senate Watergate committee, was now a senator from Tennessee.

On November 9, just six days after Republicans' poor performance in the midterms, the House Judiciary Committee held hearings concerning impeachment. Nineteen experts testified about whether the Constitution contemplates impeachment for the kinds of acts Clinton allegedly committed. The experts solicited by Republicans claimed that Clinton's behavior offered textbook examples of impeachable offenses; those summoned by Democrats claimed that impeachment was reserved for actions more egregious and more directly implicating the president's official responsibilities.

On November 13, Clinton and Paula Jones reached an agreement to settle her lawsuit, with Clinton paying Jones $850,000 but not admitting guilt. (Jones's appeal of the dismissal of her suit was pending at the time.) The White House now felt in position to put the entire affair behind it and privately supported Democrats in Congress who tried to persuade Republicans to formally "censure" the president as an alternative to impeachment. Republicans, having come too far to settle for a mere statement of condemnation, declined the overtures.

On November 19, Independent Counsel Starr testified before the Judiciary Committee. The session proved contentious, to put it mildly. Before Starr had even been sworn in, Representative Conyers called him a "federally paid sex policeman."[6]

Starr's two-hour opening statement painstakingly covered Clinton's sins, but he also exonerated Clinton with respect to various matters he had investigated before Monica Lewinsky came along: Whitewater, the so-called "Travelgate" scandal (various White House office workers being fired, allegedly to make room for friends of the Clintons), and the White House's alleged improper collection of FBI files. Starr presented himself as a pure officer of the court who sought nothing but justice: "I am not a man of politics, of public relations, or of polls."[7]

Democrats weren't buying it. In the course of his hour-long questioning of the witness, Democrat counsel

Abbe Lowell hardly asked about the evidence and allegations against Clinton. Instead, he sought to paint Starr as a partisan inquisitor, emphasizing his contacts with Paula Jones's lawyers and his failure to report possible conflicts of interest when appointed independent counsel in the first place.

Each member of the committee was allotted five minutes to question Starr. Democrats used theirs as much to speechify as to question the witness, whereas Republicans lobbed him softballs. The prime-time showdown (literally, as it aired at 8:30 p.m.) was between Starr and Clinton's personal counsel, David Kendall. Kendall, too, spent no time on the allegations against his client. Instead, he sought to prosecute Starr. Among his many accusations, perhaps the most serious was that Starr's team engaged in illegal leaking of grand jury testimony on an unprecedented scale. Starr claimed the leaks actually came from Clinton's lawyers. Impasse.

Throughout his allotted 90 minutes, Kendall dripped contempt for Starr. Republican counsel David Schippers offered a slightly different perspective. "I've been an attorney for almost forty years," he said to Starr. "I want to say I'm proud to be in the same room with you and your staff."[8]

The next day, November 20, Samuel Dash, the well-regarded Watergate investigator who had been serving as Starr's ethics adviser, stepped down from that position, claiming that Starr acted improperly by appearing as an advocate before the committee.

Shortly after Clinton's grand jury testimony, the House Judiciary Committee sent the president 81 questions to be answered under oath. On November 27, the White House delivered to the Judiciary Committee Clinton's answers, which for the most part reiterated what he had told the grand jury. His tone was defiant, any cooperation reluctant. For example, when asked whether he had taken an oath to tell the truth, the whole truth, and nothing but the truth, Clinton responded, "I do not recall the precise wording of the oath."[9]

On December 1, the Judiciary Committee heard from two ordinary citizens who had been convicted of perjury in connection with civil suits. One of them, a doctor for the U.S. Department of Veterans Affairs convicted for falsely denying sexual relations with a patient, told the committee that the president "must abide by the same laws as the rest of us."[10] If such testimony hit home, the same hearing also produced a less successful witness for the Republicans: Charles Wiggins, a senior federal court of appeals judge who had been a member of the House Judiciary Committee that recommended the impeachment of Richard Nixon. Wiggins testified that, while Clinton did commit impeachable offenses, they were "not of the gravity to remove him from office."[11]

On December 8, Clinton's attorneys opened the defense case. In his opening statement, Greg Craig acknowledged that Clinton's actions were immoral, but insisted they were not impeachable. Craig called several witnesses designed to establish that Clinton's misdeeds bore no relation to Richard Nixon's, including Richard Ben-Veniste, a Watergate prosecutor; three members of the Judiciary Committee in 1974 who voted to impeach Nixon; and William Weld, a former Republican governor who had served on the impeachment inquiry staff (alongside Hillary Rodham) during Watergate.

One of Clinton's own lawyers, Chuck Ruff, had been a Watergate special prosecutor, and now he made a closing argument for the defense. Ruff told members of the committee that they "cannot overturn the will of the people." Such language was a redundant reminder that impeachment is at least partly a political process. (Indeed during this hearing and beyond, Clinton met and spoke on the phone with several moderate Republicans, seeking their support if the case came to the full House.)

Under aggressive questioning from Republican members, Ruff skillfully set forth the Clinton line with respect to perjury: The president had been, at least in his own mind, "evasive but truthful."[12] But, Ruff implied, even if Clinton had falsified which parts of Lewinsky's body he had touched, and thus technically had been wrong to claim they did not have sexual relations under the definition used during his deposition, did Congress really wish to impeach a president over *that*?

In his closing statement, House Democratic counsel Lowell drew a dryly amusing contrast with Watergate. There, tapes proved that Nixon misused the CIA, FBI, and IRS. Here, the relevant tapes involved "Monica Lewinsky and Linda Tripp talking about going shopping."[13]

How could anyone compare the abuse of constitutional powers at the heart of Watergate with lies about a consensual private affair?

Lowell's Republican counterpart, David Schippers, advanced a drastically different view: "If you don't impeach," he told the members, "then no House of Representatives will ever be able to impeach again."[14] Perhaps Schippers did not know that, at the Andrew Johnson impeachment and trial, pro-impeachment congressmen had made the same claim.

Late in the afternoon of the next day, December 11, just as the Judiciary Committee concluded debate and was about to commence a vote on impeachment, President Clinton walked out to the Rose Garden and made a statement. He apologized more fully than ever before; he was "profoundly sorry for all I have done wrong in words and deeds."[15]

Ten minutes later, the clerk of the Judiciary Committee called the roll. The Committee approved three articles of impeachment, two charging perjury (one in Clinton's deposition in the Jones case, the other before the grand jury) and one obstruction of justice. Two of the votes went according to straight party-line vote, whereas the perjury charge stemming from Clinton's deposition in the Jones case produced a single defection (Republican Lindsey Graham voting no). The committee recessed at 9:15 p.m., leaving the vote on the fourth article for the following morning.

Article Four charged abuse of power stemming from

Clinton's numerous lies to the American people and in his answers to the 81 questions from the Judiciary Committee, as well as frivolously invoking executive privilege to impede the independent counsel's investigation. However, as this article was perceived to lack support, Republicans amended it the following morning to strike all of it except Clinton's false answers to the committee's questions. The stripped-down article passed 21–16 along straight party lines. The committee would send the full House four articles of impeachment.

During the following week, members of the House, especially those considered swing votes, received thousands of phone calls and emails. They also took note of polls showing that roughly 60 percent of the American people opposed impeachment. Democrats continued to lobby their Republican colleagues to accept the compromise of censuring Clinton, a measure approved of by a majority of Americans.

On December 16, 1998, the day before the full House of Representatives was scheduled to begin impeachment hearings, Clinton ordered commencement of a four-day cruise missile attack on Iraq. The mission was supposedly retaliation for Saddam Hussein's failure to comply with U.N. resolutions to permit inspections designed to ensure that he retained no weapons of mass destruction.

Also on December 16, David Schippers arranged for fence-sitting members of the House (and any other members who wanted to join them) to see an exhibition of evidence that, because it came in late and was inflammatory, Chairman Hyde excluded from the Judiciary Committee hearings: documents supporting the claim that 20 years earlier Clinton had raped a woman, Juanita Broaddrick. (Broaddrick did not come forward at the time, but filed an affidavit with Paula Jones's lawyers in 1997.)

On December 17, the House convened in the morning and passed a resolution 417–5 supporting the troops flying combat missions in Iraq. House Speaker-to-be Bob Livingston (anointed Gingrich's successor, though it could not become official until the next congressional session in January) announced a one-day postponement of the impeachment hearings on account of the military action. Democrats protested to no avail that the postponement should last until the military action was complete.

Livingston had other problems on his hands besides angry Democrats. That day, lured by a $1 million offer by *Hustler* publisher Larry Flynt, a woman came forward and revealed that she had an affair with Livingston years earlier. Livingston confessed to his colleagues that he had indeed "on occasion strayed from my marriage,"[16] an awkward admission just as Livingston's troops sought to impeach a president for misconduct rooted in adultery.

On Friday, December 18, at 9:00 a.m., the House of Representatives convened to consider the second presidential impeachment in U.S. history.

In the opening statement favoring impeachment, Chairman Henry Hyde immediately clarified that this "is not a question about sex" but rather "a question of the willful, premeditated, deliberate corruption of the nation's system of justice." He closed his eloquent remarks by urging the House to "keep our appointment with history."[17] He received a standing ovation . . . from the Republicans.

House minority leader Dick Gephardt opened for the Democrats and, like most Clinton defenders, did not address the specific charges against the president. Instead, he waged a series of complaints: 1) the debate should not be happening while U.S. troops were in combat; 2) the punishment of impeachment was disproportionate to President Clinton's misconduct; and 3) it was unfair that the censure option was not being brought to the floor. "You are trampling the Constitution," he scolded Republicans, and received a standing ovation . . . from the Democrats.[18]

Twelve hours of angry debate ensued, with Republicans savaging Clinton and Democrats accusing Republicans of a "coup d'état" and "constitutional assassination."

The following morning, Livingston took to the floor and called on Clinton to resign. Democrats screamed at him "*You* resign!" and Livingston proceeded to do exactly that—or, at any rate, to renounce his claim to be the next Speaker of the House. Was this real life or a Tom Clancy novel? A president on the verge of impeachment was bombing a foreign country and the impeaching party had just lost its new leader to a scandal of his own.

Both sides immediately seized on Livingston's move to support their narrative. To Republicans, he had displayed what honorable people do under such circumstances: Clinton should follow Livingston's lead and resign or else be made to leave office involuntary. To Democrats, Livingston was another victim of a growing "sexual McCarthyism" that had to stop. Neither side would get its wish.

Just a few hours after Livingston's dramatic announcement, and some impassioned pleas from both sides, the roll was called. The House of Representatives adopted two of the four proposed articles of impeachment.

The vote was 228 to 206 supporting impeachment for Clinton's perjury before the grand jury, with all but 10 members (five in each direction) voting the party line. The vote on obstruction of justice was 221–212, with all but five Democrats voting no and all but 12 Republicans voting yes. The other two articles, also based on allegations of perjury, were defeated. One, alleging falsehoods in Clinton's deposition in the Jones lawsuit, went down 229–205, with the same five Democrat yes votes and 29 Republicans breaking ranks to vote no. The other, alleging falsehoods and non-responses to the 81 questions propounded by the Judiciary Committee, was defeated 285–148, with only one Democrat voting yes and 81 Republicans in opposition.

The vote sent the case to the Senate for trial, but more immediately it sent House Democrats scurrying to 1600 Pennsylvania Avenue. Eighty of them piled into buses and cars that took them to the White House for a show of solidarity with the impeached president.

Two tickets for Bill Clinton's impeachment trial, January 14–15, 1999.

The Republicans had prevailed in the House, but polls gave them no cause to gloat. The public continued to oppose the removal of Clinton from office and showed little stomach for a drawn-out process. The House managers wanted to call at least 15 witnesses, but Senate Majority Leader Trent Lott, who held several secret meetings with pollsters and political consultants, wanted no part of that. After considerable internal debate, and then debate with the Democrats, Senate Republicans deferred the question of witnesses until mid-trial.

As this and other questions about trial procedure were negotiated among the senators, the House managers, and Clinton's attorneys, one thing was understood and from time to time articulated: There was virtually no chance Clinton would be convicted. In a private session, Senator Ted Stevens, a Republican from Alaska, told the House managers that they would be wasting their time calling witnesses, because at least 34 senators would never vote to convict. This was *Alice in Wonderland*: Verdict first, trial later.

To those who refused to consider the case a done deal (out of either excessive optimism or pessimism), the identity of the person presiding over the trial, Chief Justice William Rehnquist, gave each side cause for concern. Rehnquist was a lifelong Republican, a conservative justice appointed to the Court by Nixon and elevated to Chief Justice by Ronald Reagan. On the other hand, back in 1992 he had written *Grand Inquests*, a book criticizing the politicized impeachment of Andrew Johnson.

Whatever the chief justice's feelings about Clinton's trial, he stayed true to his own sartorial preferences. As he had for the last few years, he wore gold braids on the sleeves of his otherwise traditional black robe, homage to a Gilbert and Sullivan opera. He had witnessed a performance of *Iolanthe* in which the Lord Chancellor wore such a costume.

The trial formally commenced on January 7. Rehnquist and the senators were sworn in by 96-year-old president pro tempore Strom Thurmond, whose father was alive during the impeachment of Andrew Johnson. Following the swearing in, the first week was given over to wrangling, most of it behind closed doors, over the still-not-determined trial processes.

The trial began in earnest on January 14, with the managers' opening statements. There would be quite a few such statements—the Republicans had put together a team of 13 managers, all House members, all of whom made opening remarks.

Their addresses mixed high-minded rhetoric about the rule of law with detailed factual recitation of the president's misdeeds and clips of his many misstatements (including "I did not have sexual relations with that woman"). The first round of opening statements was effective enough that it reportedly had some Democratic senators reconsidering their opposition to conviction. The Senate recessed at 7:00 p.m.

The next day brought opening statements by five more managers and, near the end of the day, the first formal objection. Democratic Senator Tom Harkin rose to object when manager Bob Barr referred to the senators as "jurors." The managers had used the term repeatedly, but for some reason Harkin held his objection until now. Quoting from the Constitution and *The Federalist Papers*, he argued at length that the senators were really judges with a broader mandate than the term jurors implied.

Chief Justice Rehnquist agreed, and admonished the managers not to use the term. Republicans were furious, though presumably more on dubious principle (whose side was the chief justice on?) than anything else. But they decided it wasn't worth overruling Rehnquist, especially since his ruling seemed eminently defensible.

When the Senate met the next day, Saturday, January 16, the managers presented the last of their opening statements. Lindsey Graham acknowledged that "to set aside an election is a very scary thought in a democracy," but claimed the Senate had little choice—a perjurer could not be the nation's chief magistrate. He urged the Senate to "cleanse this office."[19]

The president's defense commenced on January 19, with a statement by Charles Ruff, a brilliant attorney who had been wheelchair-bound from the age of 25 (having become paralyzed through a non-diagnosed illness) and would pass away the next year. Ruff succeeded in poking holes in the managers' case, but arguably the more impressive pro-Clinton statement came later that night from the president himself, during the annual State of the Union address. Clinton actually made no mention of his trial, but earned rave reviews for his upbeat tone, bipartisan message, and even for mouthing "I love you" to his wife, who sat up in the gallery with, among others, civil rights hero Rosa Parks.

The next day brought opening statements from Clinton's attorneys Greg Craig and Cheryl Mills. The latter, an African American woman (the 13 House managers were all white men), received powerful praise from all corners. She compared Clinton to Thomas Jefferson, John F. Kennedy, and Martin Luther King Jr., great but flawed men whose sexual escapades did not detract from their commitment to human rights.

The following day, January 21, brought forth more Clinton defenders. His attorney David Kendall did a workmanlike job, but Dale Bumpers, Clinton's fellow Arkansan whose 24-year tenure in the Senate had ended with his retirement just three weeks earlier, stole the show. Most memorably, the folksy Bumpers said: "When you hear somebody say 'this is not about sex,' it's about sex."[20]

Friday, January 22, was the first of two days set aside for questions from the senators and answers by the attorneys. Senators submitted questions for one side or the other to the chief justice, who read them aloud. Many of the questions were planted by the attorneys, giving them a chance to play gotcha with factual errors by the other side. Occasionally, a question broke through the rat-a-tat-tat and got to the heart of the matter. One such question came from Robert Byrd, the crusty Democrat from West Virginia, the longest-serving senator in U.S. history and a rare Democrat considered a possible yes vote to convict Clinton.

Byrd quoted from *Federalist* 65 that impeachment redresses "the abuse or violation of some public trust" and asked Clinton's lawyers, "How does the president defend against the charge that, by giving false and misleading statements under oath, [he] abused or violated some public trust?"[21] Ruff responded that Clinton's false statements were in the context of a lawsuit over a private matter and it was absurd to believe that such misconduct is so serious as to threaten the country or justify overturning the will of the people. Apparently, the answer landed. Later that day Byrd put out a statement calling for dismissal of the charges and an end to the trial.

Another question that proved influential came jointly from Democratic senators Herbert Kohl and John Edwards. Assuming Clinton did in fact commit perjury and obstruction of justice, they asked, "can reasonable people disagree with the conclusion that . . . he must be convicted and removed from office?"[22]

Lindsey Graham responded, "Absolutely. You have to consider what is best for this nation. . . . When you take the good of this nation, the upside and the downside, reasonable people can disagree on what we should do."[23]

It was a reasonable answer, but devastating for the case against Clinton. For one thing, it was a hard sell that it is "best for the nation" to remove a president against the will of the people, who not only elected him twice but clearly (as reflected in public opinion polls) did not want him removed. For another, the very idea that "reasonable people can disagree" about whether to remove the president could be seen as good reason not to remove him. It was like the prosecutor in a criminal case telling the jury that reasonable people could disagree about whether the defendant is guilty. If so, how could the jury find guilt beyond a reasonable doubt? Since conviction and removal of a president is a last resort, undoing a democratic election, it arguably should be reserved for cases—like Nixon's—where pretty much all people of good will agree that it is necessary. Clinton's lawyers pounced on Graham's candid concession and brought it up periodically for the duration of the trial.

On January 27, the Senate voted on Byrd's motion to dismiss. It fell 56–44, a near party-line vote, with only Wisconsin Democrat Russ Feingold crossing party lines and voting against dismissal. It was a pyrrhic victory for the Republicans, insofar as it signaled that Clinton had at least 44 votes, 10 more than needed for acquittal.

That same day the Senate finally resolved key procedural issues that had been deferred: whether witnesses would be called and, if so, how many. The managers had pared down their wish list from 16 to three: Lewinsky, Vernon Jordan, and Sidney Blumenthal, the latter a White House aide who supposedly led a campaign to claim that Lewinsky stalked Clinton. By the same 56–44 vote, the Senate agreed to hear the testimony of the three witnesses.

But now Clinton's team insisted that if witnesses were called, they would need additional discovery and might call witnesses of their own for rebuttal. After much wrangling, it was agreed that the three witnesses would be deposed. If their depositions produced any surprising new evidence, the Clinton side would, by agreement of the two Senate leaders (Republican majority leader Trent Lott and Democrat minority leader Tom Daschle), be given additional time to prepare and/or call witnesses of their own.

Lewinsky was deposed on February 1 but gave the

House managers nothing useful. Indeed, she so easily fended off her questioner, manager Edward Bryant from Tennessee, that Clinton's lawyers didn't bother to question her. Manager Asa Hutchinson from Arkansas deposed Jordan the next day. Here too, nothing significant emerged. Clinton's lawyers asked just a few questions, softballs eliciting from Jordan that the assistance he gave Lewinsky in finding a job was routine, something he did for many young people, and had nothing to do with influencing her behavior with respect to the Paula Jones lawsuit. Finally, Graham and Californian Representative James Rogan questioned Sidney Blumenthal on February 3. Blumenthal denied participating in any efforts (much less efforts spearheaded by Clinton) to smear Lewinsky.

Behind the scenes, much maneuvering now occurred. Republicans knew they did not have the votes for conviction, so they pondered lesser moves. Might they finally agree to censure the president (something some Democrats supported all along)? Or settle for "findings of fact" of his guilt by majority vote? Simply adjourn without any vote? And did they want to call the three deposed witnesses to give live testimony?

As it turned out, they could not garner sufficient support for any of those options. Instead, the managers pressed ahead with the case and showed select clips from the videotaped testimony of Lewinsky, Jordan, and Blumenthal. Clinton's defense team, for its part, also showed select clips of Lewinsky's and Jordan's depositions.

On February 8, closing arguments began. After six House managers reiterated the case for conviction, Charles Ruff alone gave the White House response. The remaining seven managers spoke in rebuttal. Unsurprisingly at this point, neither side presented anything new or different. But Henry Hyde did score a clean hit in response to Ruff's charge that the managers "wanted to win too much." He replied that "none of the managers has committed perjury nor obstructed justice . . . nor encouraged false testimony before the grand jury. That is what you do if you want to win too badly."[24]

Beginning February 9, the Senate deliberated behind closed doors for three days. On February 12, they met in open session. Each senator made a brief statement, and then the roll was called. The Senate acquitted the president (on Lincoln's birthday, for whatever that's worth), which by this point was a foregone conclusion. The vote to convict was 45–55 on perjury and 50–50 on obstruction. Zero Democrats supported either article. Five Republicans voted to acquit Clinton of obstruction and 10 voted to acquit him of perjury. (Arlen Specter, an iconoclastic Republican from Pennsylvania, wanted to vote "not proved"—an option, he noted, available under the law of Scotland. He ended up declaring "not proven, therefore not guilty" on both articles.)

In a sense, the key question throughout the Clinton impeachment saga was whether the case more closely resembled that of Andrew Johnson or Richard Nixon. But, in a different sense, the most salient aspect of the Clinton case distinguished it from both the Johnson and Nixon cases: There was never a realistic chance that Clinton would be removed from office. Therefore, the national ordeal was ultimately pointless.

On the eve of the House vote on impeachment, Henry Hyde had proposed a compromise. If the Democrats dropped resistance to impeachment, he would get the Senate to agree to censure rather than convict the president. At least at that moment, Hyde was conceding that he saw impeachment as symbolic: He and his fellow Republicans would feel vindicated by a bipartisan impeachment even if it did not result in Clinton's removal from office.

One could understand Hyde's temptation. The entire Clinton case was dogged by its partisan nature. Hyde's compromise would flip the switch—suddenly, *everything* (the work of both the House and Senate) would seem bipartisan.

But impeachment is too blunt a weapon to be used to make a statement, and Hyde's proposed solution would have been short-sighted. To see why, we need to dip back to August 20, a few months before the proposed compromise. On that day, three days after his grand jury testimony, Clinton ordered the bombing of suspected terrorist sites in Afghanistan and Sudan. Immediately came accusations of "Wag the Dog"—a reference to the 1997 movie in which a president wages war to distract the nation from a scandal. Ditto when Clinton bombed Iraq on the eve of impeachment hearings. Concern that the command-er-in-chief engaged in military action for purely personal gain is terrible for the nation. Such suspicions will arise when impeachment is pursued. Suddenly, everything the president does gets seen through the impeachment lens. In addition, bitter division throughout the country is inevitable.

These things have long-term consequences. Calls to impeach Clinton's successor, George W. Bush, and his successor, Barack Obama, became commonplace (as discussed in chapter six). Payback begets payback begets payback. When a weapon of last resort becomes a weapon of first resort, the prospect of bipartisanship disappears and our entire political process suffers. Among other things, impeachment itself becomes seen as a partisan weapon rather than a constitutional safeguard. Rare cases of clearly justified impeachment will meet a stiff knee-jerk resistance.

The Clinton impeachment itself suffered from the kind of severe partisanship that has increasingly afflict-ed Congress over the last several decades. Henry Hyde wanted to avoid that. He studied the work of the Rodi-no Committee during Watergate and modeled as much as possible after the Watergate proceedings, including the format of the articles of impeachment. But despite Hyde's efforts, in one key respect the Clinton impeachment broke with precedent.

In 1973, the House Judiciary Committee employed both majority and minority staffers in drafting reports.

In 1998, that did not happen, because the Republicans thought Democratic staffers would impede committee work.

In the end, the Clinton impeachment resembled the Andrew Johnson impeachment more than the Nixon case in two crucial respects: 1) the desire to remove the president came almost exclusively from the opposition party, and 2) Clinton did not commit clearly impeachable offenses.

But there was also a critical difference between the Johnson and Clinton cases, one that made the latter a tougher case. Complaints with Andrew Johnson revolved almost completely around his resistance to Reconstruction. In other words, he was impeached over moral and political differences—an improper use of impeachment.

By contrast, those favoring Clinton's impeachment could make a conceptually tidy argument in good faith: Perjury and obstruction of justice undercut the ability of the courts to function, and are thus intolerable from the person constitutionally responsible for executing the laws of the land. If the president can break laws when it serves his purposes, what kind of message is sent? Since he enforces laws for everyone else, exempting himself amounts to hypocritical self-dealing.

The context surrounding the Clinton impeachment, however, muddied the matter. That context starts with the lawsuit by Paula Jones, which was, to put it charitably, thin. No credible evidence suggested retaliation by Clinton for whatever took place between Jones and him in a hotel room. Moreover, the underlying conduct, if any, took place years before Clinton was president—and Jones never came forward until he was president and she was encouraged to do so by his political enemies.

The immediate trigger was a magazine article in which unnamed Arkansas state troopers said that Clinton had a girlfriend named Paula. Jones claimed to have brought legal action because she felt harmed by that false allegation. However, Clinton had nothing to do with the article. Quite the contrary, the article defamed him as well as her. Yet Jones did not seek recourse against *American Spectator* magazine or the state troopers who maligned her. She took action against Clinton, who had zero to do with the allegations that infuriated her.

Moreover, Jones received financial and public relations support from organizations dedicated to destroying Clinton. (Her lawsuit was so weak that she might have had difficulty finding an attorney under normal circumstances.) In that context, Clinton found himself subject to a fishing expedition concerning women he may have been involved with, even though those relationships were at best peripherally related to Jones's allegation. Indeed, Judge Wright later ruled that everything about Monica Lewinsky was inadmissible because "not essential to the core issues" in the case. Judge Wright, a Republican appointed to the bench by George H.W. Bush, eventually dismissed the lawsuit as lacking a legal basis.

Thus, Clinton faced irrelevant questions in a baseless lawsuit that appeared politically motivated, where honest answers threatened not just his presidency but also his marriage. In that extreme situation, he engaged in evasion and a few outright lies.

Potentially more troubling was his treatment of Betty Currie, an innocent person whom he arguably encouraged to lie—albeit, again, to defend himself from a baseless and ill-motivated lawsuit that threatened his presidency and marriage. But if he wronged Currie, it was not a wrong against the nation, certainly not in Clinton's capacity as president.

Clinton told lie upon lie, some under oath. Judge Wright, despite dismissing Jones's lawsuit, fined him $90,000 for contempt of court, and both the Arkansas Bar Association and United States Supreme Court suspended his license to practice law. These punishments were just. One can disapprove of Clinton's impeachment without condoning his actions.

The case for impeaching Clinton, while not frivolous, was not compelling. It represents a middle ground in between the Johnson and Nixon cases. Taken as a trio, the three cases offer valuable lessons to which we turn in chapter six. First, we consider one other vehicle besides impeachment for removing an unfit president.

FIVE

"Unable to Discharge"

When arguing that impeachment does not require a criminal act, commentators give examples they consider obvious. Suppose the president was perpetually drunk or went AWOL for a prolonged period. Such conduct, though not criminal, would clearly warrant removal from office. However, the examples are more problematic than they may seem.

As we have seen, one can effectively commit crimes (as in "high crimes and misdemeanors") against the Constitution without necessarily violating specific laws. Richard Nixon's misuse of government agencies provides a perfect example. But drunkenness? It seems at a minimum a stretch—and maybe even a category mistake—to consider that a "crime" by any definition.

And yet, commentators on impeachment always insist that neglecting one's presidential responsibilities would indeed constitute an impeachable offense. This conclusion has a firm pragmatic basis: A drunken or otherwise obviously unfit president must be replaced, and impeachment was historically the only available vehicle for doing so. Stretching normal language seemed a reasonable price to pay to produce a result necessary for the nation's well-being. The fault lay in the failure of the original Constitution to provide for removal of a president who is unfit but has committed no grievous offense.

Actually, the original Constitution did address what happens when the president is unable to do the job, but only as part of a broader provision governing what happens when the president is removed. Article I, Section 2, Clause 6 provides: "In Case of the Removal of the President from Office, or of his Death, Resignation, *or inability to discharge the Powers and Duties of the said Office*, the same shall devolve on the Vice President, and the Congress may by Law provide for the Case of Removal, Death, Resignation or Inability, both of the President and Vice President, declaring what Officer shall then act as President, and such Officer shall act accordingly, until the Disability be removed, or a President shall be elected."

This provision served two purposes: 1) It established that the vice president takes over upon a president's permanent removal (through conviction, death, or resignation) or temporary removal due to a "disability." 2) It empowered Congress to establish a further line of succession in case there is no vice president when the president is removed. It left two major gaps, however.

First, while addressing what happens when the presidency is left vacant, and authorizing Congress to address a dual president/vice president vacancy, it failed to address a vacancy of the *vice president only*. As a result of this omission, the position would remain vacant. Second, while anticipating the situation in which the president is disabled, and providing that the vice president temporarily takes over, Article I, Section 2, Clause 6 said nothing about how this would work. Who determines that the president suffers such a disability? Who determines that he has sufficiently recovered to resume the powers of the office?

It is not as if these questions didn't occur to the framers. At the Constitutional Convention, Delaware delegate John Dickinson succinctly posed exactly the right questions about the disability clause: "What is the extent of the term 'disability' and who is to be the judge of it?"[1] But no one had answers, and the delegates elected to let the matter slide.

The oversight with respect to a vice presidential vacancy may have stemmed from the sense that the office lacked importance. Its first occupant, John Adams, called the vice presidency "the most insignificant office that ever the invention of man contrived or his imagination conceived."[2] The 32nd vice president, John Nance Garner, more colorfully declared the office "not worth a bucket of warm piss."[3]

But the vice president *is* important, if only because he is a heartbeat away from the presidency. Or, as Adams put it with characteristic shrewdness and uncharacteristic brevity: "I am nothing but I may be everything."[4] With the "everything" in mind, it is strange to think that, throughout U.S. history, the vice presidency frequently stood vacant—on 17 occasions, there was no vice president for an extended period of time. We saw, in connection with Andrew Johnson, the absence of a vice president as problematic: The president pro tempore of the Senate, Ben Wade, Johnson's political enemy, stood next in line (by virtue of the succession statute passed in 1792) if Johnson were removed. Related problems surfaced throughout U.S. history. There have been many periods of vice presidential vacancy during which the president pro tempore, as well as the Speaker of the House (who was next in line), belonged to a different party than the president.

Johnson's impeachment dramatized these problems, but he was by no means the first president to be without a vice president. James Madison saw two of his vice presidents die in office and served without an underling for three years. There was a period in Madison's second term when he fell ill and speculation arose that he might die, to be succeeded by the elderly and frail Vice President Elbridge Gerry. If Gerry then passed away (which in fact he did the following year), the presidency could not have passed to the president pro tempore of the Senate because the latter position was vacant after Madison appointed William Crawford Minister to France. Next in line was House Speaker Henry Clay, who was reviled by many allies of Madison.

Since Madison survived, so did this constitutional infirmity. A few decades later, John C. Calhoun resigned the vice presidency in December 1832 to become a U.S. senator, and President Andrew Jackson finished his term without a vice president. Two decades after that, when

John Tyler became president upon the death of William Henry Harrison just 40 days into his term, the vice presidency remained vacant for four years. Ditto from July 1850, when Millard Fillmore assumed the presidency upon the death of Zachary Taylor, until March 1853. Just one month into the term of Fillmore's successor, Franklin Pierce, Vice President William King passed away, leaving Pierce with no vice president for virtually his entire term.

So, too, the deaths of the vice president left the office vacant for various stretches during the Hayes, Cleveland, McKinley, and Taft administrations. Three other presidents—Coolidge, Truman, and Lyndon Johnson—assumed the office upon the death of their successor, and thus had no vice president of their own until the next election.

From George Washington's presidency through Lyndon Johnson's, there were vice presidential vacancies totaling 38 years—roughly 20 percent of U.S. history up to that point. Fortunately, though, a double vacancy never occurred: No president ever died (or otherwise left office) during the period without a vice president,* despite a few close calls. John Tyler was aboard a warship when an artillery gun exploded, killing six people, including the secretary of state and secretary of the navy. Franklin Pierce

---

* The line of succession after the vice president was established by statute, beginning in 1792, and changed in 1886 and 1947. Currently, in the event of double vacancy the Speaker of the House becomes president, followed by the president pro tempore of the Senate, then the secretary of state and other cabinet heads.

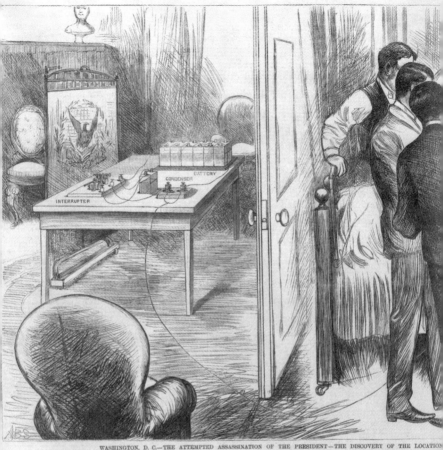

WASHINGTON, D. C.—THE ATTEMPTED ASSASSINATION OF THE PRESIDENT—THE DISCOVERY OF THE LOCATION

suffered a severe bout of malaria that briefly threatened his life.

If the absence of a vice president was a problem from the beginning, the other constitutional gap, an incapacitated president, did not surface for almost a century. (A partial exception was James Madison's illness, a three-week period during which he cancelled meetings and did

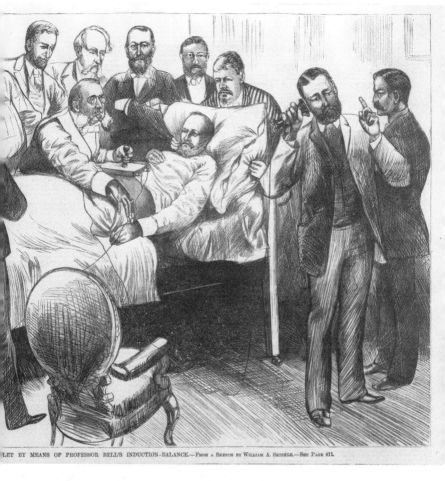

LET BY MEANS OF PROFESSOR BELL'S INDUCTION-BALANCE.—From a Sketch by William A. Skinkle.—See Page 411.

little but recuperate.) In 1881, however, the constitutional lacuna loomed large. On July 2, President James Garfield was struck by an assassin's bullet at the Baltimore and Potomac Railroad Station in Washington D.C., and clung to life for almost three months before succumbing. Despite intermittent signs of recovery, Garfield was in no condition to work, even apart from his frequent bouts of hallucination. He conducted a single piece of presidential business—signing an extradition paper—during this period before passing away on September 19. During the attempted recovery he was a good distance from the White House, bed-ridden in a home on the New Jersey shore.

Throughout this period of Garfield's incapacity, the United States effectively had no president. Vice President Chester Arthur did immediately come to Washington after Garfield's shooting; he stayed there for 10 days and held meetings with the cabinet. But when Garfield's condition stabilized, Arthur returned home to New York, where he remained in relative seclusion and conducted no official business. He neither visited nor communicated with the president.

Garfield's cabinet members attended to their business, keeping the government going, but obviously lacked the power to take many official actions, including conducting foreign policy. Concerned by this situation, in August Secretary of State James Blaine drafted a memorandum arguing that Arthur should come to the capital and assume the powers of the presidency. Only a few cabinet members agreed. Arthur himself, who was from the opposite wing of the Republican Party as Garfield, feared being accused of usurpation. It was an understandable concern, given that Garfield's assassin had shouted, "Arthur is president now!"

Garfield's death mooted the issue, and during Arthur's presidency the nation again went without a vice president. Three months into his administration, Arthur sent a message to Congress raising the relevant issues concerning an incapacitated president:

> Is the inability [referred to in the Constitution] limited in its nature to long-continued intellectual capacity or has it a broader import? What must be its extent and duration? How must its existence be established? Has the President whose inability is the subject of inquiry any voice in determining whether or not it exists, or is the decision of that momentous and delicate question confided to the Vice-President, or is it contemplated by the Constitution that Congress should provide by law precisely what constitutes inability and how and by what tribunal or authority it should be ascertained? If the inability proves to be temporary in its nature, and during its continuance the Vice President lawfully exercises the functions of the Executive, by what tenure does he hold his office? Does he continue as President for the remainder of the four years' term? Or would the elected President, if his inability should cease in the interval, be empowered to resume his office?[5]

Arthur's interest in these questions stemmed not only from his experience as vice president during Garfield's incapacitation, but also from his own health issues: He suffered from a usually fatal kidney condition. However, despite occasional bouts of nausea and depression, Arthur served out his term in passable health and the issue of an incapacitated president receded.

Just eight years after Arthur left office, in May 1893, President Grover Cleveland was diagnosed with a malignant tumor in his mouth. During what was presented to the public as a vacation cruise on a yacht, Cleveland in fact had his tumor removed by a team of surgeons in a tiny, poorly lit room. Only one cabinet member even knew about the surgery. Vice President Adlai Stevenson was also kept in the dark. In July, Cleveland took another cruise for the purpose of follow-up surgery. This time, though, word leaked out, and in August a Philadelphia newspaper reported Cleveland's medical operations. Most of the press denounced the story as fake news.

The incapacitation problem next surfaced on October 2, 1919, when Woodrow Wilson suffered a stroke that left him largely disabled for the last 16 months of his term. His condition was kept secret from the press and public. Secretary of State Robert Lansing privately suggested that Vice President Thomas Marshall be called in to execute presidential powers, but the idea was vetoed by Wilson's right-hand man, Joseph Tumulty. Lansing also raised the issue at a cabinet meeting, but received little support. His proposal went nowhere, and Marshall, who like Chester Arthur wished to avoid any suggestion that he usurped the president's power, took no initiative. Tumulty and Wilson's wife Edith effectively ran the country for the duration of Wilson's term. Lansing did call periodic cabinet meetings until Wilson (who recovered somewhat and was sentient) fired him for overreaching in February 1920.

During and in the immediate aftermath of Wilson's presidency, members of Congress introduced various pieces of legislation to deal with the incapacity problem, which would have given the Supreme Court, Congress, or the cabinet the power to declare a president disabled and temporarily replace him (with the vice president or someone else). The House Judiciary Committee considered these options but never reached a consensus. As was the case when James Blaine and Chester Arthur raised the issue in the wake of the Garfield shooting, the matter eventually faded without any action taken.

The issue again surfaced when Dwight D. Eisenhower suffered a heart attack on September 24, 1955, and doctors prescribed a month of complete rest. Vice President Nixon, Chief of Staff Sherman Adams, and the cabinet adopted a "committee system" which more or less maintained business as usual at the White House, and fortunately, no crisis arose requiring presidential action. Nixon later described the problematic situation: "Aside from the President, I was the only person in government elected by all the people; they had a right to expect leadership, if it were needed, rather than a vacuum. But any move on my part which could be interpreted, even incorrectly, as an attempt to usurp the powers of the presidency, would disrupt the Eisenhower team."[6]

The problem resurfaced twice more during

Eisenhower's presidency. On June 9, 1956, he underwent relatively minor surgery to remove an obstruction of the small intestine. For two hours the president was anesthetized and unconscious. Eisenhower lamented that, for those two hours, the nation—a nuclear superpower engaged in a cold war with another nuclear superpower—lacked a commander-in-chief. He asked the Department of Justice to study the problem and recommend a solution, and asked his cabinet for their input in a meeting in February 1957. The cabinet kicked around various ways of handling a president's incapacity, but reached no consensus. On November 25, 1957, Eisenhower suffered a stroke. Though he recovered quickly, the episode revived concern about the incapacitation problem.

Actually, even before Eisenhower's heart attack in 1955, House Judiciary chairman Emanuel Cellar of New York asked the committee's staff to study the presidential disability issue. The staff distributed to judges, academics, and public officials a questionnaire seeking views on all aspects of the question, including whether a constitutional amendment was needed. Respondents offered numerous takes on these questions but no consensus was reached.

In 1957, Attorney General Herbert Brownell proposed to the committee a constitutional amendment: The president could declare his own inability, or, if he was unable to, the vice president and a majority of the cabinet could do so. In either event, a written declaration by the president of his recovery would enable him to resume his authority.

Members of Congress raised potential problems with this approach. For example, what if the president stubbornly and prematurely declared his recovery? Brownell replied that impeachment would be available, but the answer was unsatisfying: Impeachment seemed reserved for cases of wrongdoing, not disability. Meanwhile, in a *New York Times* op-ed, former President Harry Truman offered a different solution—creation of an elite medical commission that would report to Congress, which by two-thirds vote of both houses could remove the president for the duration of his term.

After another Eisenhower illness in 1958, another subcommittee was formed and held hearings, this time under the auspices of the Senate Judiciary Committee. This subcommittee ended up approving a version of the plan proposed by Attorney General Brownell the previous year, but Congress would not pass it.

Meanwhile, an increasingly alarmed and sickly Eisenhower decided to take unilateral action. He released a letter to the public on March 3, 1958, explaining that he had given Nixon the authority to determine if and when he (Eisenhower) was disabled and he (Nixon) would need to take over. Eisenhower reserved for himself the right to determine when he had recovered sufficiently to reclaim the powers of the office. His successors Kennedy and Johnson informally maintained the same understanding with their vice presidents.

This solution made good sense but lacked the force of law. If the unofficial but de facto president gave orders, must anyone obey them? Not really. Would his signature on a bill make it law? No.

At least in retrospect, it is surprising that the dual problems of vice presidential vacancy and presidential incapacity went unsolved for so long. Irreversible momentum toward a solution was finally created by the assassination of John F. Kennedy on November 22, 1963. Kennedy's successor, Lyndon Johnson, who had a history of heart trouble, served the duration of Kennedy's term without a vice president. The assassination not only reminded everyone of that recurring situation but also refocused attention on the problem of presidential incapacity. The next day, in the *New York Times*, James Reston observed that "for an all too brief hour today it was not clear again what would have happened if the young President, instead of being mortally wounded, had lingered for a long time between life and death, strong enough to survive but too weak to govern."[7]

The new president himself shared the newspaper's concerns. Just a month after he took the oath of office, Johnson wrote a letter to Speaker of the House John McCormack codifying an oral agreement the two apparently had reached in which, should Johnson become incapacitated, McCormack would resign as Speaker and become acting president. Johnson would resume the powers of the office upon his own determination that he was able to do so.

The problem of potential disability was again compounded by the absence of a vice president. Though

Johnson designated McCormack as his temporary re-placement-in-waiting, the Speaker was 72 years old and generally not regarded as presidential timber. Next in line, president pro tempore of the Senate Carl Hayden, was 86.

The problems of presidential disability and vice presidential vacancy again took center stage, and assorted constitutional amendments were proposed. The ensuing Senate hearings produced the usual disagreement about how to handle the incapacity situation, but there was an emerging consensus that provision must be made to fill vice presidential vacancies. Everyone felt there should be someone who sees himself and is seen by others as wait-ing in the wings in case the president dies or otherwise leaves office—ideally someone who, like the president, was elected by the entire country. In other words, the nation needs a vice president at all times: The frequent vacancies were intolerable.

Though nothing was done to fill Lyndon Johnson's vice presidential vacancy, after his election with running mate Hubert Humphrey in 1964 the cause was again tak-en up. In his January 1965 State of the Union address, Johnson urged Congress to pass laws "to insure the nec-essary continuity of leadership should the President be-come disabled or die."[8] Senator Birch Bayh proposed a constitutional amendment shortly thereafter, and in a statement to Congress on January 28, Johnson endorsed it. The proposed amendment worked its way through each house of Congress, then a conference committee, and in July a final version was adopted and sent to the states, where three-fourths had to ratify it to make it part of the Constitution. On February 10, 1967, Minnesota and Nevada put the 25th Amendment to the Constitution over the top.

The amendment, whose seeds were planted by Eisenhower's attorney general Brownell a decade earlier, simultaneously resolved the vice presidential vacancy and presidential incapacitation problems. (The amendment's conformity to Brownell's approach was no coincidence; he chaired an American Bar Association Committee that drafted an early blueprint of the amendment.) It easily fixed the frequently recurring problem of vice presidential vacancies by providing that "whenever there is a vacancy in the office of the Vice President, the President shall nominate a Vice President who shall take office upon confirmation by a majority vote of both Houses of Congress."

It didn't take long for this provision to pay dividends: Had it not been in place, there would have been no vice president during the impeachment proceedings against Richard Nixon, following Spiro Agnew's resignation on October 10, 1973. The person next in line, Speaker of the House Carl Albert, was not considered—including by himself—prepared to become president. To make matters worse, he was a Democrat. Had Nixon not nominated and Congress not confirmed Gerald Ford as vice president, Republicans would have been less willing to proceed with impeachment and, later, push for Nixon's resignation. The 25th Amendment thus paved the way for Nixon's removal—and for stability in its aftermath, especially since Ford had been overwhelmingly confirmed as next in line, and since he, in turn, immediately nominated Nelson Rockefeller to be the new vice president. Rockefeller, too, was fairly quickly and easily confirmed.

As House Judiciary Chairman Peter Rodino said at the time, "It is unquestionable that without section 2 of the 25th Amendment, this nation might not have endured nearly so well the ordeal of its recent constitutional crisis."[9]

Sections Three and Four addressed presidential incapacitation. Section Three stated that the vice president assumes the powers of the president whenever the president gives Congress a written declaration that he cannot discharge the powers and duties of the office. The president reclaims the responsibilities of the office through a similar declaration. This provision has been used successfully several times for short-term transfer of power when presidents have undergone general anesthesia for minor surgical procedures—in 1985 when President Reagan had polyps removed from his colon and in 2002 and 2007 when President Bush underwent colonoscopies.

Section Four addressed the situation in which the president is too incapacitated to write such a letter. In such a situation, the transfer of power to the vice president occurs when he and a majority of the president's cabinet ("or of such other body as Congress may by law provide") write to Congress declaring the president's incapacity. Once again, the temporary transfer lasts until the president issues a written declaration reclaiming his powers, but this time with a wrinkle.

The drafters of the 25th Amendment anticipated the situation in which the vice president and Congress believe the president incapacitated whereas the president believes himself still up to the job. If the president disputes the claim of incapacity, or later claims to have regained capacity, the vice president and Congress have four days to express disagreement. Then Congress has three weeks to decide the issue, with the president keeping or reclaiming power unless two-thirds of both houses agree that he is in fact disabled.

Two points about the 25th Amendment warrant emphasis. First, it envisions that reasonable disputes about the president's capacity will be resolved in his favor. This is also somewhat true with respect to removal via the impeachment process, insofar as two-thirds of the Senate is required to convict an impeached president. However, only a bare majority of the House is needed to impeach the president. When it comes to a disputed removal via the 25th amendment, two-thirds of *both* houses are required. Clearly, the drafters of the 25th Amendment did not wish for the vice president and the president's cabinet to remove the president through a backdoor that circumvented Congress. Instead, they made it *more* difficult to use the 25th Amendment than impeachment.

Second, the 25th Amendment covers situations involving mental as well as physical inability. The drafters had foremost in mind a situation such as the stroke that befell Woodrow Wilson or the bullets that struck John F. Kennedy—that is, a physically disabled president. But they borrowed Article I, Section 2's broad language ("unable to discharge the powers and duties of his office"), which covers a wider range of situations. There could be cases, such as the president being perpetually intoxicated or slipping into dementia or mental illness, that require his removal without him having committed a grievous offense. The 25th Amendment speaks to that situation.

This straightforward interpretation of the language is buttressed by the history of the amendment's adoption. Its architect, Senator Bayh, and other senators, made clear that mental disabilities were also within its scope, that they had in mind any inability to perform the constitutional duties of the office.

The issue received renewed attention when the *New York Times* published Ross Douthat's column "The 25th Amendment Solution for Removing Trump" on May 16, 2017, suggesting that the 25th Amendment, not impeachment, offers the best vehicle for dealing with concerns about President Trump's unfitness. Douthat began by making a general observation of attributes that any president needs: "a reasonable level of intellectual curiosity, a certain seriousness of purpose, a basic level of managerial competence, a decent attention span, a functional moral compass, a measure of restraint and self-control." Douthat suggested that deficiency in any of these areas could render a president unfit, then applied his analysis to the current president, beginning with the assertion that President Trump is childish.

> It is a child who blurts out classified information in order to impress distinguished visitors. It is a child who asks the head of the F.B.I. why the rules cannot be suspended for his friend and ally. It is a child who does not understand the obvious consequences of his more vindictive actions—like firing the very same man whom you had asked to potentially obstruct justice on your say-so.
>
> A child cannot be president. I love my children; they cannot have the nuclear codes. But a child also cannot really commit "high crimes and misdemeanors" in any usual meaning of the term. . . .
>
> Which is not an argument for allowing him to occupy that office. It is an argument, instead, for using a constitutional mechanism more appropriate to this strange situation than impeachment: the 25th Amendment to the Constitution. . . .
>
> The Trump situation is not exactly the sort that the amendment's Cold War–era designers were envisioning. He has not endured an assassination attempt or suffered a stroke or fallen prey to Alzheimer's. But his incapacity to really govern, to truly execute the serious duties that

fall to him to carry out, is nevertheless testified to daily—not by his enemies or external critics, but by precisely the men and women whom the Constitution asks to stand in judgment on him, the men and women who serve around him in the White House and the cabinet.

Read the things that these people, members of his inner circle, his personally selected appointees, say daily through anonymous quotations to the press. (And I assure you they say worse off the record.) They have no respect for him, indeed they seem to palpitate with contempt for him, and to regard their mission as equivalent to being stewards for a syphilitic emperor.

. . .

This will not get better. It could easily get worse. And as hard and controversial as a 25th Amendment remedy would be, there are ways in which Trump's removal today should be less painful for conservatives than abandoning him in the campaign would have been—since Hillary Clinton will not be retroactively elected if Trump is removed, nor will Neil Gorsuch be unseated. . . .

Meanwhile, from the perspective of the Republican leadership's duty to their country, and indeed to the world that our imperium bestrides, leaving a man this witless and unmastered in an office with these powers and responsibilities is an act of gross negligence, which no objective on the near-term political horizon seems remotely significant enough to justify.[10]

Unsurprisingly, Douthat's column met with major resistance, and not just from supporters of the president. Rather, many people thought Douthat mischaracterized the role of the 25th Amendment, which cannot be brought into play to remove a president who is wholly sentient and whose capacities are no different from when he was elected.

But while the 25th Amendment may indeed be unrealistic under such circumstances, Douthat made several important points. First, the president's incapacity may not manifest in high crimes and misdemeanors. Second, a president may not be up to the job for reasons unrelated to a stroke or other physical infirmity. Third, the president's unfitness may be *worse* when it involves an ongoing condition than if he committed a particular crime. It may make him a frightening steward of the nation's nuclear arsenal, where there is little room for error. For all of these reasons, if we find ourselves with such a president, the 25th Amendment does seem to be the most proper— indeed the only—vehicle for his removal.

It may seem inconceivable that a president's own vice president and cabinet would remove him under any circumstance short of a major physical infirmity. After all, even when Presidents Garfield and Wilson *were* physically disabled, their vice presidents avoided filling the vacuum for fear of being tagged usurpers. However, that was before the 25th Amendment constitutionalized such "usurpation" to safeguard our national well-being. Yes, the vice president and cabinet will be reluctant to invoke the 25th Amendment absent physical disability, but that very fact legitimizes the amendment's usage: Surely, if the president's own cabinet asserted his or her inability, the circumstance would be so dire that the public would likely accept the judgment.

As with impeachment, only more so, the Constitution provides built-in safeguards, especially the requirement of support for removal by two-thirds of both houses if the president contests the initiative. This, too, would supply legitimacy, since it virtually guarantees that members of the president's own party in Congress (along with a majority of his own cabinet) concur that he or she cannot be allowed to stay in power.

SIX

LESSONS

We noted in the introduction Santayana's famous remark that those who cannot remember the past are condemned to repeat it. But, of course, remembrance alone is not enough. We must also learn from experience. History offers many lessons when it comes to removing the president, including the following.

Lesson 1
IMPEACHMENT IS A LAST RESORT

Impeachment can be habit-forming. Especially since the Clinton administration, there has been a growing tendency to call for impeachment upon the first significant dissatisfaction with a president. But the trend began even before Clinton. A lamentable side effect of Watergate was that people began to see impeachment as a strategic weapon to be wielded against a president one dislikes rather than an option of last resort to be used against a president who demonstrates unfitness.

Calls for the impeachment of Nixon's successor, Gerald Ford, began almost immediately, with his decision to pardon Nixon just one month into his presidency. Twelve years later, seven Democratic congressmen introduced a resolution to impeach Ronald Reagan over the Iran-Contra affair.

The Clinton ordeal quickened the reflex to reach for impeachment. Throughout the second term of his successor, George W. Bush, Democrats in the House introduced resolutions supporting impeachment stemming from the Iraq War and assorted other misdeeds. Some of these efforts acquired traction, especially a resolution in June 2008 proposing 35 articles of impeachment.

The charges covered not only the war, but also an effort to overthrow Iran's government; the mistreatment of detainees in the Terror Wars; the inadequate response to Hurricane Katrina and global warming; the outing of CIA agent Valerie Plame; alleged tampering in the 2004 election; and efforts to destroy Medicare, among other things. By a vote of 251 to 166, the House referred the resolution to the Judiciary Committee, though the expiration of Bush's term soon rendered action moot.

The calls for impeachment came even faster and more furiously during the Obama presidency. Back in 2010, political commentator Jonathan Chait predicted that, by the end of Obama's time in office, the House would vote to impeach him. Though the prediction proved inaccurate, the reasoning was sound and scary. "What will they impeach him over?" Chait asked. "You can always find something. Mini-scandals break out regularly in Washington."[1]

Indeed, although formal articles of impeachment against Obama were never introduced, by the end of his second term members of Congress and others had called for his impeachment on numerous grounds: the false claim that he was born outside of the United States; the killing of four U.S. embassy personnel in Benghazi; his executive orders on immigration; the IRS allegedly targeting conservative groups; an executive order allowing transgendered students to use boys or girls bathrooms; and much more. It wasn't just partisan Republicans. In 2014, noted civil libertarian Nat Hentoff floated the idea of impeaching Obama over his use of executive orders pertaining to domestic spying.

As the litany of charges against both Bush and Obama should make clear, many of the calls for impeachment reflected political disagreements and/or claims of incompetence rather than high crimes and misdemeanors as traditionally understood. People now invoke the "I" word whenever a president does something they strongly dislike.

This trend accelerated with the election of Donald Trump. Books by respectable journalists urged the impeachment of both Bush and Obama, but not until their second terms. The first book to advocate Trump's impeachment came out in April 2017, less than three months after he took office. The first call for Trump's impeachment on the floor of Congress came just four months into his administration.

This is regrettable. Impeachment should be a last,

not first resort. To be sure, the temptation to see impeachment as a convenient means of getting rid of the other guy dates back to the early days of the Republic. When the Democrat-Republicans impeached Supreme Court Justice Samuel Chase in 1804, Senator William Giles candidly explained the purpose: "We want your office in order to give it to a better man."[2]

But we already have a vehicle for putting better people in office: elections. If we don't like federal judges, the solution is to elect better presidents and senators to do the appointing and confirming. If we don't like the president, defeat him after four years or wait out the expiration of his second term. The foremost virtue of democracy lies in the resort to ballots rather than bullets to determine our representatives. True, impeachment itself involves ballots rather than bullets, but that is small comfort to the citizen who sees 50 million ballots nationwide trumped by 220 in the House of Representatives and 67 in the Senate. When people get the idea that their votes don't matter, it may not be long before they ponder less peaceful alternatives.

Violence aside, we don't want people to feel that their voices and votes are ignored. A demoralized, alienated citizenry cannot be healthy. Of course, some disappointment in the democratic process is inevitable, both because elected officials aren't angels and because power corrupts. These truths prompted the framers to craft safeguards, including impeachment. But quick resort to impeachment is a remedy worse than the problem. It will leave people feeling not just disillusioned but disenfranchised.

The United States already suffers from uncommonly low voter turnout, which is in part a function of people believing that their vote makes no difference.

The great constitutional theorist Charles Black, who assisted Thurgood Marshall in drafting the brief to the Supreme Court that prevailed in the landmark case *Brown v. Board of Education*, was militant about racial issues and despised the "Southern strategy" that helped elect Richard Nixon. He strongly disapproved of Nixon. But when Black authored *Impeachment: A Handbook* in early 1974, as Nixon's crimes were becoming apparent, he was unwilling to advocate impeachment. To the contrary, Black insisted that, before impeachment be undertaken, "it is essential that absolute bedrock legitimacy be inarguably present."[3] His assessment recalls the maxim: "When it is not necessary to change, it is necessary not to change." However one regards this sentiment in general, the preference for a default condition of inaction makes great sense when it comes to the drastic remedy of impeachment. When it is not necessary to impeach, it is necessary not to impeach.

If impeachment is a last resort, what circumstances suggest that the last resort has arrived? The answer to that question involves several considerations discussed below, but one in particular should always be considered: Will the president again face the voters? Impeachment will generally be more appropriate during the president's second term than first for the simple reason that the voters themselves can effectively impeach the first-term president. The People, after all, are sovereign in U.S.

democracy and capable of making the judgment that the president has rendered himself unfit. And, yes, they can interpret the Constitution. They, no less than members of Congress, can determine the meaning of "high crimes and misdemeanors."

There are, however, two crucial exceptions to the preference for letting the voters decide the fitness of a president. First, a president's misconduct may involve stacking the deck in his own favor with respect to his re-election. That could occur in many situations beyond the obvious cases of voter fraud or suppression. The "dirty tricks" the Nixon campaign engaged in against his prospective or actual opponents would mark an exception to "let the voters decide," since precisely what the campaign was doing was improperly interfering with that decision process. Ditto if the president knowingly violates the First Amendment, since fair elections require free speech and a free press.

Second, if the president's alleged high crimes and misdemeanors suggest that he poses a major threat—for example, that he might recklessly commence a nuclear attack. There may be cases where the urgency of the threat posed by an unfit president mitigates against waiting for election results. Where the threat is imminent, however, the 25th Amendment provides the faster remedy.

Lesson 2
IMPEACHMENT REQUIRES HIGH CRIMES AND MISDEMEANORS

The House should impeach, and the Senate convict, only when they can point to a specific action or pattern of actions that meets the constitutional standard. Put more crudely, the president may *not* be impeached for doing a lousy job.

We could imagine a system that did in fact permit removal of our chief executive simply for inadequate performance. Such a system exists in some countries—elections can be called at any time and/or a legislative vote of "no confidence" can remove an unpopular leader. But that is not and never has been the U.S. form of government. The founders emphatically rejected such a system. As noted in chapter one, James Madison objected to presidents serving "at the pleasure of the Senate." His fellow Virginian, George Mason, explained that allowing the president to be "the mere creature of the legislature" would be a "violation of the fundamental principle of good government."[4] Certainly it would be a violation of U.S.-style democracy.

We needn't blindly follow the framers, but there are obvious advantages to the approach they gave us, with presidents serving four-year terms absent disqualifying acts that meet a high constitutional hurdle. More frequent turnover would breed dangerous instability. While this is not the place to trumpet the advantages of American democracy over alternatives, for present purposes we must only observe that we do not have a system that allows for removing the chief executive any time and for any reason. If we wish to move in that direction, we should do so only after extensive debate and the passage of appropriate constitutional amendments.

There are several reasons why impeachment is the wrong vehicle for changing the American way and subjecting the president to recall whenever Congress so desires. First, Congress is supposed to impeach and convict only if the president commits treason, bribery, or other high crimes and misdemeanors. To use "high crimes and misdemeanors" as justification for removing any president one dislikes would make a mockery of language.

Second, Congress now has a body of precedents built up around actual impeachments. In the Johnson, Nixon, and Clinton cases, it was generally understood and acknowledged that the president could not be removed absent high crimes and misdemeanors (or treason or bribery). To abandon such precedents would render those cases useless as guidance for when a particular president should be accused and removed. It would leave us unmoored, with each Congress making it up as it goes.

Third, within our structure of government, impeaching and removing the president absent specific and serious wrongdoing wouldn't make sense. When the government replaces a leader via a vote of "no confidence" in a parliamentary system, a new government gets formed, typically around a coalition led by a different party. Not so in the United States. The president will be replaced by the vice president, a member of his own party. Whatever benefit may have accrued if Al Gore replaced Bill Clinton, it would have made little sense as part of a movement to change the course of government.

But even if Gore would have taken the nation in the direction Republicans preferred, impeachment still would have been inappropriate. In the case of Andrew Johnson, conviction and removal would indeed have produced a change in direction, as Democrat Johnson would have been replaced by Radical Republican Ben Wade. It was no coincidence that the Radical Republicans selected Charles Sumner and John Bingham as managers in the Senate trial, or that Thaddeus Stevens emerged as a leading voice for conviction—these men were passionate abolitionists and, as discussed in chapter two, the effort to remove Johnson was really about Reconstruction. History has treated Sumner, Bingham, and Stevens well but has been unsympathetic to their effort to oust Johnson. The lesson is clear: Even the most profound moral and political objections to the president do not justify impeachment.

Sumner openly admitted that he saw impeachment as a vehicle for changing the nation's approach to Reconstruction. His written report after the Johnson trial said: "It is very wrong to try this impeachment merely on the articles. It is impardonable to higgle over words and phrases" while the president's actions produce "terrible, heart-rending consequences." Sumner acknowledged that Johnson's real crime had nothing to do with the firing of Edwin Stanton as Secretary of War. He wrote that

Johnson's "usurpation with its brutalities and indecencies" was apparent by the end of 1866—before the Tenure of Office Act was even passed. Lest there be doubt, Sumner clarified that "plainly he ought to have been impeached and expelled at that early day."[5] In that same vein, Benjamin Butler argued that any behavior "highly prejudicial to the public interest" is impeachable.[6]

In other words, crimes and misdemeanors be damned. But this also means the Constitution be damned and the U.S. form of democracy be damned. Whatever our misgivings at any moment, our form of democracy has on balance worked well. The Radical Republicans were right on the issue that divided them from Johnson but wrong to think that a president's dereliction merits impeachment absent a specific impeachable offense.

At the ballot box, voters ask themselves whether the country would be better served by a new president and new direction. Members of Congress may also ask that question as part of the impeachment inquiry, but first they must ask whether the president has committed an impeachable offense. Unless they can honestly and in good faith conclude that he has, the inquiry should go no further.

There is only one exception to the rule that removal of the president requires treason, bribery, or high crimes and misdemeanors. As discussed in chapter five, if the president is incapacitated, he may be temporarily removed regardless of whether he has committed any impeachable offense.

Lesson 3
IMPEACHMENT REQUIRES UNFITNESS

Just as a president may not justly be impeached without having committed treason, bribery, or other high crimes and misdemeanors, he ought not be convicted and removed *solely* because he committed such an act. Rather, in addition to the judgment that he committed an impeachable offense, the Senate should make the additional judgment that he is unfit to remain in office.

As a practical matter, this means we should allow room for the president to remain in office when he has committed a single error and shows sincere contrition. Indeed, the very act of recognizing and taking responsibility for an improper action may call into question the idea that the president is unfit. In such a case, if the president is clearly up to the job in terms of knowledge and intellect, removing him would be questionable.

In general, impeachment should not be a game of gotcha where Congress can establish that the president committed an offense, unless the offense is exceptionally serious. If the offense is aberrational, and acknowledged by the president, and if there is no reason to think him unfit, the drastic step of impeachment should generally be avoided.

Lesson 4
IMPEACHMENT REQUIRES POPULAR SUPPORT FROM THE AMERICAN PEOPLE.

At a press conference shortly after he had resigned as

attorney general rather than fire Archibald Cox—the beginning of the Saturday Night Massacre that led to Richard Nixon's downfall—Eliot Richardson was asked about impeachment. He gave a curious answer: "That's a question for the American people."[7]

The questions of whether to impeach and convict the president are on their face constitutionally reserved for the House and Senate respectively—not the U.S. citizenry. But, as Richardson understood, members of Congress are rarely oblivious to public opinion, particularly in their state or district. They will not stop reading their mail during an impeachment process. You might as well ask them to stop breathing.

In that sense, to say that impeachment requires the support of the American people is just an unavoidable reality. Richard Nixon and Bill Clinton provide a pair of cases in point: Nixon found himself on the verge of impeachment when and only when his popularity tanked and polls showed overwhelming public support for his removal. Clinton survived his Senate trial because the country opposed his removal.

But the notion that Congress should not impeach a popular president (absent truly exceptional circumstances) is not a mere circular claim that Congress should not do what it would not do anyway. After all, Clinton *was* impeached despite the public's opposition. This is less surprising than it may seem. Many Republican House members lived in districts that favored impeachment. So too, many senators lived in states that favored conviction.

But, conditioned though they are to consider the views of their constituents, here is a case where members of Congress should look at the bigger picture. The fact that U.S. citizens *overall* opposed impeachment and removal counseled against pushing the process to the brink. Public opposition to removal saved Clinton, but we never should have reached that point. Impeaching the president against the public's desire is generally a bad idea.

For that reason, citizens should freely voice their opinions about impeachment. Here, I disagree with Charles Black, the revered law professor whom I quoted approvingly earlier. In his book on impeachment, Black wrote that the citizens' role in the impeachment process is "vigilant waiting." Why should citizens be mere spectators at this crucial constitutional moment? Because, Black observed, impeachment "is confided by the Constitution to responsible tribunals."[8] But that could equally be said about passing laws. That too is delegated to Congress. Does it follow that citizens should not make their views on legislation known?

The Constitution sets forth a standard ("high crimes and misdemeanors") that requires interpretation. Perhaps Black felt that constitutional interpretation is beyond a layperson's capacity. But here we benefit from the teaching of one of Black's students at Yale Law School, Akhil Amar, one of the nation's preeminent constitutional law scholars. Amar has repeatedly explained that the framers expected ordinary citizens to interpret the Constitution. At the founding, juries were considered sufficiently well versed in law, including constitutional law, to decide cases based on their interpretations—for example, refusing to convict a defendant if they thought the law in question was unconstitutional.

The ideas of "jury review" and "jury nullification" have fallen into disuse. (We've come to expect judges to decide questions of law, and juries only questions of fact.) Regardless of how one feels about those issues, we ought not expect citizens to defer 100 percent to members of Congress when it comes to "high crimes and misdemeanors." Unlike judges, members of Congress are not experts on the Constitution. And the citizenry, not they, are the ultimate sovereign in our democracy. We the People ordained and established the Constitution. We, not the government elites who serve and represent us, own the document and the democracy it set in motion and governs.

Of course, in the very drafting of the Constitution, the People delegated many tasks to government officials, including impeachment. And, for practical reasons, it could hardly be otherwise. The full citizenry cannot conduct an impeachment inquiry or trial. But to go to the opposite extreme, and say that citizens should not express opinions or that Congress should ignore such opinions, contradicts the spirit of our democracy and is itself impractical.

Lesson 5
IMPEACHMENT AND REMOVAL MUST BE BIPARTISAN
Impeachment will never be completely bipartisan, either

in the Congress or with the people at large. Even Richard Nixon, at the bitter end, had the support of roughly 25 percent of the U.S. people and supposedly could have counted on 10 to 15 votes to acquit in the Senate. But Nixon would have been impeached and convicted, and the American public would have accepted the result, because so many Republicans supported it. Such bipartisanship is essential.

Once again, we have a "lesson" that may seem to be merely descriptive of reality. Congress will generally *need* bipartisan support to remove a president, since one party rarely controls two-thirds of the Senate. However, that isn't necessarily the case. The Republicans did control two-thirds of the Senate in 1868, and would have removed Andrew Johnson but for some defections. But they *shouldn't* have. If they had persuaded the Seven Tall Men to stay small and convict, it would have been a bad thing. I don't mean simply that Johnson did nothing warranting impeachment, though that is true. Rather, the fact that there was no Democratic support was itself a powerful reason to avoid removing Johnson—for two reasons.

First, impeachment requires, if not certainty, at least a high level of confidence. When *no one* in the opposition party in Congress favors impeachment, the situation calls for humility. Republican senators during the Clinton impeachment should have asked themselves (and a few perhaps did): "If this situation really called for Clinton's ouster, wouldn't at least *one* Democrat favor it?"

Of course, the senator who asked himself that may

have concluded that the Democrats were unanimously mistaken. But even that conclusion should, as a brute fact, give our hypothetical Republican senator pause. Assuming one party has the numbers to convict on a purely partisan basis, would that be good for the country when it practically guarantees that the opposing party would view the action as a de facto coup d'état? One that means they will likely try to impeach your president when they return to power?

Note that the problem of a partisan impeachment can arise even when there is no risk of a partisan conviction. While typically neither party will enjoy two-thirds advantage in the Senate, one party will always enjoy majority power in the House, and that party need not be the same as the one in the White House. Because impeachment, unlike conviction, requires only majority vote, the prospect of partisan impeachment will often be present. It should be resisted, for the same reason that a partisan conviction should be resisted—it is likely unwise on the merits and always divisive in practice. If the effort to remove the president is doomed to fail in the Senate, it will likely not be worth the bitterness and divisiveness it causes along the way.

Lesson 6
IMPEACHMENT MUST PASS THE SHOE TEST

Senators at an impeachment trial take an oath to do "impartial justice." To which one might reply, "What other kind is there?" And yet, as we have discussed, it is unrealistic to expect politicians to provide the kind of impartial justice we expect from judges. Politicians face voters and rarely ignore the fact. Virtually all politicians in the United States belong to one of two political parties in a binary system where one party's gain is the other's loss. The fate of the member of Congress is often tethered to that of the president of his or her party, and varies inversely with the fate of an opposing president. On matters of impeachment, then, we cannot expect members of Congress to fully shed their partisanship any more than they can shed their skin.

This is true not just in theory but also in practice. The one major thread connecting the three presidential impeachment sagas is the large degree of partisanship, with substantial bipartisanship found only at the tail end of the Nixon impeachment process.

But while we must accept and even embrace the fact that politicians will engage in politics, it does not follow that members of Congress should behave as naked partisans in the impeachment process, that they are as free to indulge their party-driven preferences as they are when, say, voting on who will be the Speaker or on allocation of office space or, for that matter, on ordinary legislation.

How can we get members of Congress to treat the impeachment process with greater impartiality while recognizing that they will never approach pure impartiality? How can we reconcile the political reality of a necessarily somewhat partisan process with the recognition that too much is at stake for members simply to vote along party lines?

One answer is for members of Congress to apply the "shoe test." Before deciding either for or against impeachment or conviction, each member of the House or Senate should ask herself a straightforward question: How would I view this case if the shoe were on the other foot—that is, if the president belonged to the opposite party? If they would not impeach or convict a president of their own party for the identical conduct, they should not do so to a president of the opposing party. Conversely, if they would impeach or convict an opposing president, they should be willing to do the same to their own.*

It is a test many members have implicitly failed during the three presidential impeachment episodes. Imagine if the Radical Republicans who impeached and nearly convicted Andrew Johnson had asked themselves: "Would we remove a president of our party for discharging a secretary of war in possible violation of the Tenure of Office Act?" An affirmative answer would not pass the giggles test, never mind the shoe test. The same question posed to those

---

* In his book on impeachment, Cass Sunstein arrives at much the same principle, though he calls the principle "Neutrality." Borrowing from the political philosopher John Rawls, Sunstein proposes that we put ourselves behind a veil of ignorance when approaching questions of impeachment, pretending we know nothing about the president except the acts he committed. Cass Sunstein, *Impeachment: A Citizen's Guide* (Cambridge MA: Harvard University Press, 2017), pp. 14–15.

who defended Richard Nixon would yield the same result. Few Republicans would have tolerated a Democratic president who abused power as blatantly as Nixon.

The Clinton impeachment presented an even clearer case of members of congress flunking the shoe test. It is hard to disagree with this assessment by Richard Posner: "One just *knows* that if the shoe were on the other foot— if everything were the same except that the President was a Republican—the Republicans would have denounced the investigation in the same terms that the Democrats used."[9] And probably vice versa as well. Many Democrats who pounded Ken Starr would have applauded if his target had been a Republican president. While Posner was talking only about the investigation, his point extends to the impeachment and trial as well. It seems safe to say that most of the Republicans who voted for impeachment and removal would not have done the same had a Republican president done what Clinton did, whereas many Democrats would have voted to impeach and remove the hypothetical Republican Clinton.

That is not to say that members of Congress were consciously hypocritical. People rationalize mightily. They may convince themselves that they would in fact vote X or Y if the shoe were on the other foot even in cases where they would not. The fact that the shoe test is difficult to apply does not make it any less important. At a minimum, the question ought to be asked, and answered as truthfully as possible.

Lesson 7

IMPEACHMENT MUST BE FOR THE GOOD OF THE NATION

Even if one can check all the boxes discussed above—if the president committed an impeachable offense, if he is unfit, there is nationwide support for his removal and bipartisan support in Congress, and impeachment and/ or conviction will pass the shoe test for a given member of Congress—one may still resist if, because of unusual circumstances, removing the president would be bad for the country.

This may be a matter of timing. Just as the House postponed the Clinton impeachment proceedings for a day when the United States bombed Iraq, it might, under certain circumstances, postpone them indefinitely if the country were at war. (Of course, a president should not be rewarded with postponement if he or she deliberately starts a "wag the dog" war precisely to achieve that result.) So too, suppose Congress discovers the president's impeachable offense with only days or weeks left in his term. It may be futile or counterproductive to set in motion the impeachment machinery at that late date. (That said, it may be that a late-date impeachment usefully enforces norms of behavior without the risk of undoing the effects of an election.)

There may be any number of other circumstances, too, in which Congress might exercise restraint, such as the nation being in the midst of a crisis and the vice president considered unqualified.

In criminal law, the jury has the power to "nullify" the

facts or law and acquit someone who clearly is guilty of a crime. Significantly, we give juries *unreviewable* powers to find a defendant not guilty. If the jury convicts someone, he or she may appeal. But, on account of constitutional protection against double jeopardy, the government may not appeal a conviction. The practical effect, and perhaps even the idea behind double jeopardy, is that juries have the power to acquit whenever justice so requires—even if the letter of the law does not. We do not want that power exercised routinely, but rather reserved for special circumstances.

The same holds true for impeachment, with "the best interests of the country" substituted for "justice" to a particular defendant. By making the Senate's decision in the impeachment trial nonreviewable, the Constitution ensures that senators can take into account the best interests of the nation. Even if the normal criteria point to conviction and removal of the president, senators must ask themselves whether some reason exists why such a decision would unduly damage the nation.

Lesson 8

TIE GOES TO THE PRESIDENT EXCEPT WHEN HE HAS FORFEITED THAT PRESUMPTION

Members of Congress might also apply what we could call the Graham test after Lindsey Graham's inadvertent assist to President Clinton. Graham, you'll recall, acknowledged that reasonable people could disagree about whether Clinton's actions warranted removal. Some thought it followed that conviction could not be justified, as any reasonable doubt should be resolved in favor of avoiding the radical action of removing the president. Another way of thinking about this is the time-honored rule in baseball that a tie goes to the runner. Tie (or even a close call) goes to the president—a corollary of the earlier lesson that impeachment is a last resort to be utilized only when clearly necessary. When in doubt, don't throw him out.

However, there is a crucial exception to this proposition, what we might crudely call the "rotten store" factor. At one point during the Nixon impeachment process, Representative Paul Sarbanes, a Democrat from Maryland, explained to a reporter his support for impeachment. It was, he said, like sifting tomatoes in a vegetable store and finding that one after another was rotten. When you try other vegetables and find the same thing, at some point you ask, "What kind of a store is this?"[10] Sarbanes, like many of his colleagues, decided that the Nixon White House was a rotten store—replete with lies and withholding of evidence, pervasive paranoia and obsession with retaliation against adversaries, "dirty tricks" against political opponents, and other suspicious behavior that could not be proven, such as the cause of the 18½-minute gap in a potentially key tape.

Such rottenness alone is not a basis for impeachment absent a proven impeachable offense. But gray areas will arise. Identifying whether particular acts constitute an impeachable offense is more art than science, and there will be cases of borderline high crimes and misdemeanors. In addition, even if members of Congress are satisfied that such an offense has been committed, they may in unusual cases determine that the nation is best served by allowing the president to serve out his or her term.

In either of these scenarios—borderline impeachable offenses or a clear impeachable offense that may nevertheless not warrant removal because of surrounding circumstances—one's vote may be influenced by an overall assessment of the administration. Was the misconduct anomalous or was it part of a host of inappropriate behavior? Has the administration earned the benefit of the doubt or the reverse? Has the president acknowledged wrongdoing and shown contrition? It is appropriate, if not inevitable, that the overall tenor of an administration will come into play in close cases.

Lesson 9

IF ALL THE ABOVE CONDITIONS ARE MET, REMOVAL IS NOT ONLY JUSTIFIED BUT ALSO MANDATORY

During the Nixon crisis, Congressman John Anderson, an Illinois Republican who six years later would do surprisingly well as a dark horse candidate for president, reflected on a generational divide in attitudes toward impeachment: "Younger people see [it] as a method of rejuvenation; older people think of it and tremble."[11]

Both perspectives make good sense. To remove a duly elected president is a far-reaching move with profound consequences. It should be done only if necessary.

It requires that an unfit president commit an impeachable offense, that there be bipartisan and public support to remove him, and no significant mitigating circumstance. But when these conditions are met, the president *must* be removed, and his removal should be seen as rejuvenating—use of an explicit constitutional remedy to sustain our constitutional democracy.

I have emphasized throughout the risk of impeachment undertaken too lightly. This perspective stems in part from the availability of other means of preventing tyranny. Thanks to the original Constitution in combination with the 22nd Amendment, a president can serve at most four years without facing the voters. We can generally wait out the president. But we should not ignore the risk in the opposite direction—underrating the damage an unfit president can do in that time.

I have said that when it is not necessary to impeach, it is necessary not to impeach. Sometimes, though, it is necessary to impeach. When such circumstances present themselves, we must demand from our servants in Congress bold and decisive action.

Lesson 10
DITTO THE TWENTY-FIFTH

What I have just said about impeachment applies equally to the 25th Amendment. To say the 25th Amendment should not be invoked lightly is an understatement. But to say that it can never be used absent physical disability is an overstatement. It should never be invoked unless it is truly necessary, but where it is necessary, *not* invoking it would be the height of irresponsibility.

Clearly, under the Constitution, if the president has committed no impeachable offenses, but is unfit, his vice president and cabinet may remove him. Especially in an era when the president controls weapons of mass destruction that can end the world as we know it, we can safely go further. If the president is unable to discharge the powers and duties of his office, which entails the ability to make rational decisions, he *must* be removed.

SEVEN

THE CASE OF TRUMP

As a special counsel is investigating possible wrongdoing by our 45th president, Donald Trump, we can apply the lessons derived from the history of presidential impeachments to the present historical moment. Of course, it is difficult to say anything definitive. At this writing we do not know what Special Counsel Robert Mueller will report about collusion between the Trump campaign and Russia, or obstruction of justice with respect to the Russia investigation.* We do not know what information other investigations of Trump (and his personal lawyer, Michael Cohen) will yield, or what new facts may be unearthed by the media.

---

* Some commentators have emphasized that there is no specific crime of "collusion" in the federal code. While this is true, it is not directly relevant to the impeachment inquiry because, as repeatedly noted, a formal crime is not necessary for impeachment purposes. However, to avoid confusion, I will avoid the word "collusion" henceforth, referring to "coordination" or other synonyms for collusion.

President Donald Trump

Accordingly, all we can do is address the principal allegations against President Trump and consider whether, if they turn out to be true, they justify impeachment and removal. We start with the one that gave rise to the appointment of the special counsel.

COORDINATING WITH RUSSIA

Robert Mueller was appointed to investigate ties between the Trump campaign and Russia, in particular the possibility that Russia or Russians conspired to help Trump win the 2016 presidential election. That Russians did in fact perpetrate covert operations to influence our election, including hacking into the e-mails of Hillary Clinton's campaign staff and disseminating embarrassing material, using droves of false social media accounts, and illegally spending millions in online advertising, has been determined by multiple United States intelligence agencies. (It is illegal for non-citizens to make campaign contributions or independent expenditures in U.S. elections.) The full extent of Russia's covert activities, and the degree to which Trump and his staff knew about, encouraged, or assisted them, remain open questions.

Several members of the Trump campaign had contacts with Russians that they initially denied. These include Michael Flynn, briefly Trump's national security adviser until he was forced to resign and later indicted by Mueller precisely because he falsely denied such contacts. In addition, we know about an exchange of e-mails between Donald Trump Jr. and an attorney with ties to the Russian government who assured him that the Russians had damaging information about Clinton. Trump Jr. replied, "I love it."[1] A meeting subsequently took place involving that attorney, Trump Jr., President Trump's son-in-law and close aide Jared Kushner, and Paul Manafort, then chairman of the campaign. (Manafort was subsequently convicted for various federal offenses, though none of the charges were directly connected with the Trump campaign.)

We know, too, that candidate Trump called on Russia to "find Hillary's e-mails"—likely in jest, but at a minimum showing an alarming insouciance about foreign involvement in a U.S. election.[2] He also refused to criticize Russia's dictator, Vladimir Putin, even resisting pointed invitations to do so. For example, when confronted by talk show host Bill O'Reilly with the fact that "Putin is a killer," the candidate replied, "There are a lot of killers. We have a lot of killers. You think our country is so innocent?"[3] A candidate who did not hesitate to criticize prisoners of war (saying of John McCain, "I like soldiers who weren't captured")[4] and gold star mothers, among many others, seemed unable to muster harsh words for a former KGB operative and present-day dictator antagonistic to the United States.

Unusual behavior toward Russia continued after Trump's election (though intermixed with the imposition of sanctions for Russian misconduct). Trump publicly questioned the findings of numerous U.S. agencies that Russia had interfered with the 2016 presidential election, and seemed to accept at face value Putin's self-serving denials. He called the Russian dictator to congratulate him for winning what most observers considered his own sham election, something Trump's advisers allegedly urged against.

Allegations that a presidential campaign worked with a foreign adversary to affect the outcome of a U.S.

election cannot be pooh-poohed. Elections are the life-blood of democracy. If they aren't free, neither are we. Of course, not all "coordination" with a foreign government would constitute impeachable conduct. Suppose, for example, a presidential candidate openly urged a foreign leader to support him based on the mutual interests of their two nations, and the leader's support consisted of public declarations of his or her preference for that candidate. This might be unseemly, but American voters could make that judgment for themselves.

The problem is graver where coordination is covert (and all the more so when it involves illegal activity, such as hacking the computers of opponents or exploiting social media in ways that may violate campaign finance laws). Covert coordination could subject the president to manipulation or coercion by an adversary, since revelations might be devastating to him.

At the Constitutional Convention in 1787, James Madison observed that the impeachment option was necessary because, among other evils, the president "might betray his trust to foreign powers."[5] Fellow delegate Gouverneur Morris echoed this concern, noting that a president "may be bribed by a greater interest to betray his trust; and no one would say that we ought to expose ourselves to the danger of seeing the first Magistrate in foreign pay without being able to guard against it by displacing him."[6]

In sum, complicity in a foreign government's operations against our elections is a close cousin of treason and certainly a basis for removing a president.

This conclusion might seem to go without saying, except some have suggested that conspiracy with the Russians would not be impeachable because it involved behavior that preceded Trump's term in office. That view is surely mistaken. Even if pre-office behavior generally cannot justify impeaching a president, there must be an exception where his improper activity helped get him elected. Otherwise, candidates could achieve office illegitimately, then thumb their noses at critics and declare that it is too late to do anything about it.

A few judges have been convicted for behavior that preceded their tenure in office, including one fairly recently. In 2010, the Senate convicted Judge Thomas Poreteus by a vote of 96–0 on four articles of impeachment, three of which involved conduct preceding his term as a federal judge. Significantly, one of Porteus's offenses involved making false statements to the Senate and the FBI in connection with his confirmation. Unless that is ground for removal, nominees would know that they could lie their way into office and safely remain—just like a president whose improper actions facilitated his or her election.

But what happens if Trump's family members and campaign aides worked with the Russians while Trump himself knew nothing about it? On the one hand, it seems that a president should not be impeached because of the misconduct of subordinates. In his aforementioned book about impeachment, Professor Charles Black put it plainly: "We have to remember that it is the *president* who must be found guilty of 'high Crimes and Misdemeanors.'"[7] The most upright presidents have had corrupt subordinates. Even George Washington lost a cabinet member to scandal.

But, as Professor Black went on to say, "The president (like anybody else) is totally responsible for what he commands, suggests, or ratifies."[8] If campaign aides coordinated with Russia at Trump's urging, or with his approval, even if the latter was given only with a wink or knowing nod, he himself is effectively guilty of working with an adversary to affect a U.S. election. Indeed, if Trump knew about his campaign's coordination with Russia, and did not demand that it cease, he committed an impeachable offense regardless of whether he affirmatively expressed approval of the misconduct.

Professor Black also noted that "when carelessness is so gross and habitual as to be evidence of *indifference* to wrongdoing, it may be in effect equivalent to ratification of wrongdoing."[9] Or as then-Congressman James Madison put it, the president is responsible for the conduct of his executive branch subordinates and must be "subject to impeachment himself, if he suffers them to perpetrate with impunity high crimes and misdemeanors against the United States, or neglects to superintend their conduct, so as to check their excesses."[10]

It is worth noting, in this connection, that one of the articles of impeachment against Richard Nixon, adopted by the House Judiciary Committee, cited his "failing to act when he knew *or had reason to know* [of] his close subordinates" acting improperly. Deliberate ignorance is no defense. If Trump did not know about his campaign's improper actions because he did not want to know, preferring to maintain deniability while not discouraging shenanigans, and his nonchalance encouraged his aides to engage in wrongdoing, he could be held responsible.

One might plausibly counter that creating an environment in which subordinates feel free to cultivate foreign interference is too vague a charge to justify impeachment. If faced with this question, members of Congress would have to decide, based on all the available evidence, whether the wrongdoing by the campaign could fairly be traced back to actions (or inaction) by the president.

Caution is in order about removing a president absent confidence in his complicity, but such caution must be mitigated by a consideration specific to the "tainted election" context. Let us suppose, hypothetically, that the Russians not only attempted to tip the 2016 presidential election with the assistance of the Trump campaign, but succeeded—in other words, Trump might have lost but for their efforts. Under that circumstance, we effectively had an illegitimate election. Yet, apart from impeachment, the Constitution offers no remedy for this obviously unacceptable situation: It contains no provision for contesting a presidential election or calling for a new one after the president has been sworn in.

Accordingly, if covert foreign operations help elect

a president, that candidate illegitimately wins while our democracy loses. If, however, the candidate's campaign engaged in wrongdoing, the presumption against impeachment must be balanced against the need to preserve the legitimacy of our electoral system. If Trump's family and aides worked with Russia in an effort to win the election, Congress should give careful consideration to how to respond, even absent proof implicating Trump directly. Under normal circumstances, the president should get the benefit of the doubt. But a president who takes office on account of foreign interference abetted by his own campaign may not be so entitled.

OBSTRUCTION OF JUSTICE

Whether or not the Trump campaign conspired with Russia's covert operations to tip the 2016 presidential election, evidence suggests that members of the campaign and later the White House staff impeded investigations into such allegations. Donald Trump Jr. apparently made false statements about his meeting with a Russian lawyer, and the president apparently helped draft a misleading statement about the meeting. And, according to President Trump himself, he fired FBI director James Comey in part because of Comey's persistence in investigating such allegations.

If conspiracy with Russia's attacks occurred, obstruction of justice may seem redundant—the underlying offense would justify impeachment even without a cover-up. But the question arises as to what happens if no underlying misconduct can be demonstrated. We often hear the adage that the cover-up may be worse than the crime, but can there be a cover-up with *no* crime? The answer is yes. Perhaps some members of the Trump campaign or administration did not know whether other members coordinated with Russia's espionage, and wanted to make sure that U.S. investigators did not find out either. Alternatively, they may have wished to prevent disclosure of activities that, while not involving crimes, were embarrassing. Regardless of motivations, anyone who knowingly impeded an official investigation—whether by the FBI, Congress, or the Office of the Special Counsel—potentially obstructed justice. If President Trump himself obstructed justice, that is surely ground for impeachment. In fact, obstruction of justice was the basis for articles of impeachment against both Nixon and Clinton.

Of course, the alleged obstructions by Nixon and Clinton were not equivalent: Nixon's concerned investigation of a burglary by his election committee, Clinton's his relationship with Monica Lewinsky. One could reasonably believe that any obstruction by Clinton with respect to a private matter did not rise to the level of an impeachable offense. The potential obstruction of justice by Trump resembles Nixon's more than Clinton's, insofar as the underlying investigation concerned covert foreign operations against the United States and an illicit effort to manipulate the 2016 presidential election.

Trump's potential obstruction of justice involved a range of actions. According to former FBI director

Comey, at a meeting attended by many principals, Trump cleared the Oval Office of everyone else so he could privately ask Comey not to prosecute Trump's former national security adviser, Michael Flynn. President Trump also allegedly enlisted leading intelligence officials to publicly deny the existence of evidence of coordination with Russia during the 2016 election.

Trump defenders have observed that the president, as the head of the executive branch, not only has the authority to *request* that the FBI director drop a particular investigation, but could lawfully *order* him to do so. Similarly, the president has virtually unlimited discretion to fire the FBI director or anyone else under him in the executive branch. As noted in the introduction, Trump's attorney, John Dowd, insisted that the president cannot obstruct justice because he is the chief law enforcement officer under the United States Constitution.

This may be true as far as it goes. As a general proposition, the president cannot be criminally charged for exercising power given to him by the Constitution, even after he leaves office. (There may be exceptions—for example, if the president accepts bribes in connection with the exercise of his or her authorized powers.) In this case, President Trump cannot be prosecuted for firing James Comey or otherwise impeding an executive branch investigation. But that does not immunize him from impeachment. As we have discussed, a president can commit an impeachable offense without violating the law.

To be clear, just because the president has the power

to do X does not preclude him from being impeached for doing X if he exercises his powers for illegitimate reasons. For example, the president has the constitutional authority to pardon everyone who is in prison, or to refuse to speak with any foreign leaders, but few dispute that such exercises of constitutional authority could be legitimate grounds for impeachment.

This point requires emphasis because it is a subset of a larger issue, sometimes framed as whether the president is "above the law." No one is *above* the law. To say that the president generally cannot be criminally charged with obstruction of justice is not to place him above the law; it *is* the law—the Constitution gives the president authority to make executive branch decisions, and thus such decisions, by themselves, cannot constitute crimes. (Though again, the president who accepted a bribe to issue a pardon or take other action could be charged with bribery after he left office.) But the more important point is that, even if the law insulates the president from criminal punishment for exercising the powers of his office, there remains a constitutional remedy when he abuses those powers: impeachment.

If the facts unearthed suggest that President Trump fired James Comey because the latter pursued a legitimate investigation, or tried to prevent him from doing so through other means, and took such actions solely to protect himself or his political allies, such actions would indeed constitute impeachable offenses.

The same holds true, only more so, if Trump fires

Special Counsel Mueller. Department of Justice regulations dictate that the special counsel can be removed only due to "incapacity, conflict of interest, or other good cause," and only by the attorney general—or in this case the assistant attorney general, Rod Rosenstein, since Attorney General Jeff Sessions has recused himself from the Russia investigation. But Trump has reportedly considered circumventing these regulations. He could fire Sessions and/or Rosenstein, expecting the replacement to fire Mueller.* Or, as head of the executive branch, he could order whoever at the Department of Justice (DOJ) is in charge of the special counsel investigation to revoke the DOJ regulations creating the office and then to fire Mueller without the need for good cause. Any action designed to derail Mueller's investigation, however, would justify impeachment unless Mueller has acted improperly or the president has another legitimate reason rooted in the national interest. If a president prevents a prosecutor from doing his or her job because he feels threatened, he obstructs justice indefensibly.

It is true that President Nixon was not impeached

---

* The DOJ regulation would still require good cause for the attorney general or acting attorney general to fire Mueller. During Watergate, a similar regulation safeguarded Special Prosecutor Cox from discharge absent "extraordinary improprieties." When several members of Congress brought suit following Cox's removal, a federal judge in the District of Columbia declared the discharge illegal. The court of appeals ruled the matter moot when Nixon resigned.

for the firing of Special Prosecutor Cox (although the Saturday Night Massacre increased calls for impeachment and may have marked a decisive moment in Nixon's downfall). However, Nixon's new attorney general appointed another special prosecutor to replace Cox. If Trump replaced Mueller with someone equally independent, the case for impeachment could be reduced, at least if he could articulate a reasonable basis for the move.

ABUSE OF THE PARDON POWER

President Trump's pardon of his political supporter, former Arizona sheriff Joe Arpaio, has been cited as a basis for impeachment. To a lesser extent, his pardon of Lewis "Scooter" Libby, a former adviser to Vice President Dick Cheney, has also been deemed problematic by some commentators. In order to determine the propriety of these pardons, we need to consider the scope and purpose of the pardon power, which requires placing it within its larger constitutional context.

Reflecting the commitment to individual liberty and protection against tyrannical government, the drafters of the Constitution provided a number of shields before an individual can be punished for violating United States law. First, a grand jury must find a probable violation of a preexisting law that made sufficiently clear that the conduct in question was forbidden. A trial judge must then allow the case to go forward, a jury must find guilt beyond reasonable doubt, and the judge must determine that the jury's verdict is supported by the evidence. Only after all that may the United States brand someone a criminal. Even *then*, the defendant may avoid punishment if the president decides to offer clemency.

Article 2, Section 2, Clause 1 gives the president "power to grant reprieves and pardons for offenses against the United States, except in cases of impeachment." Apart from the impeachment exception, the president's power to pardon is absolute, but it does not follow that all pardons are acceptable. A president who pardons someone in exchange for a cash gift clearly could be impeached. He or she would have committed bribery, an explicitly impeachable offense. (A governor, Oklahoma's J.C. Walton, was in fact impeached and removed in part for selling pardons.) Even pardons that violated no laws could be impeachable. As emphasized, legal behavior may constitute high crimes and misdemeanors for constitutional purposes. Conceivably, Richard Nixon violated no laws when he asked the IRS to harass his opponents. Presidents have the authority to instruct the IRS, just as they have the power to issue pardons, but exercising such authority contrary to the spirit of justice and rule of law may trigger impeachment. So too with pardons: A particular pardon may be improper, notwithstanding the president's authority to issue it. But when is a pardon improper?

The principal purpose of the pardon power is clear: It promotes justice and mercy. Sometimes a trial judge or jury gets it wrong. Sometimes they get it right at the time, but new circumstances arise that put the decision or sentence in a different light. And at times, the feeling arises that the defendant justly sentenced has nevertheless suffered enough.

Alexander Hamilton's discussion in *Federalist* 74 reinforces the justice and mercy rationale. Hamilton endorsed the "benign prerogative of pardoning" because "the criminal code of every country partakes so much of necessary severity that without an easy access to exceptions in favor of unfortunate guilt, justice would wear a countenance too sanguinary and cruel."[11] This elevated language expresses a straightforward idea: The law can be too harsh in particular cases. Hamilton's phrase "unfortunate guilt" captures the person either innocent, or guilty but with extenuating circumstances. In the former case, the pardon reverses injustice. In the latter case, Hamilton says, the pardon provides "a mitigation of the rigor of the law," showing "the mercy of the government."[12] But it isn't just justice and mercy. Beyond doing right by the individual involved, pardons can serve the public interest. For example, Hamilton cited pardons to defeated insurgents and rebels that could "restore the tranquility of the commonwealth."[13]

The very first use of the president's pardon power, by Hamilton's boss George Washington, dovetails with

---

* In that same vein, in an 1833 Supreme Court opinion, Chief Justice John Marshall termed the pardon "an act of grace." A Court opinion in 1855 called it "an act of mercy flowing from the fountain of bounty and grace." *United States v. Wilson*, 32 US 150 (1833) [after "an act of grace"]; *United States v. Athens Armory*, 35 Ga. 362 (1855) [after "an act of mercy"].

Hamilton's senses of its purposes. After the army put down the Whiskey Rebellion, Washington pardoned all the rebels who had violently protested against the whiskey tax. They had committed acts of arson and even tarred and feathered tax collectors, but Washington understood that they got carried away in the face of a threat to their livelihood. When pardoning them, he explained that he felt the need to show "every degree of moderation and tenderness" that would not jeopardize national safety, especially when doing so would promote national reconciliation.[14]

Other founding fathers were similarly merciful against people whose understandable passions or fears got the better of them in the public arena. John Adams pardoned those involved in Fries's Rebellion, and Thomas Jefferson and James Madison pardoned deserters from the Revolutionary War and the War of 1812, respectively.

Beginning in roughly 1885, presidents regularly gave reasons for their pardons. On occasion, they cited the likely innocence of the man convicted, usually established by new evidence. More typically, they felt the recipient of the pardon had suffered enough. Often presidents cited the man's sickness or his family's dependence on him. Other recurring justifications for pardons included youth or old age, illness, and pregnancy.

In addition, presidents continued to make postwar pardons for their healing effect on the nation. In a 1927 Supreme Court case upholding President Taft's commutation of a death sentence, Justice Oliver Wendell Holmes wrote that a pardon amounts to the president's determination "that the public welfare will be better served."[15] Gerald Ford defended his pardon of Richard Nixon on that basis, claiming the nation would have suffered from the criminal prosecution of Nixon, both because he (Ford) would have been consumed by the matter and because it would have reopened ugly wounds. Ford also noted that Nixon, as the only president ever forced from office by scandal, had suffered enough.

Justice, mercy, and the public interest thus were and are the main bases for pardons. The problem is that pardons can produce *injustice* rather than justice and harm rather than benefit the public interest. Alexander Hamilton recognized as much, lamenting the use of the pardon "to shelter a fit object of [law's] vengeance."[16] This will happen, Hamilton suggested, when the president indulges in favoritism, bending to his own biases or the beseeching of others.

What does all of this tell us about President Trump's pardon of Sheriff Joe Arpaio? Arpaio violated a federal district court order that he stop detaining individuals solely based on the belief that they were in the country illegally, a practice that many thought involved racial profiling. As a result, following a bench trial he was convicted of criminal contempt. President Trump pardoned Arpaio prior to sentencing, and a White House statement explained the basis of the pardon:

Throughout his time as sheriff, Arpaio continued his life's work of protecting the public from
the scourges of crime and illegal immigration.
Sheriff Joe Arpaio is now 85 years old, and after
more than 50 years of admirable service to our
nation, he is a worthy candidate for a Presidential pardon.[17]

The statement does not defend Arpaio's underlying
criminal acts, nor suggest that punishment would be too
severe. (He faced a maximum term of six months.) It
does make reference to his age, which could be seen
as gesturing toward mercy, but the statement suggests
the pardon primarily was a reward for public service,
an aim that does not comport with the usual rationales
behind the pardon power. President Trump viewed Arpaio as an ally in the fight against illegal immigration,
not to mention a vocal political supporter. Accordingly,
we should recall Hamilton's warning against use of the
pardon power as an act of favoritism. Moreover, Trump's
decision to pardon Arpaio raises separation of powers
concerns insofar as Arpaio's crime was contempt of the
judicial process and his underlying action impeded the
judiciary's effort to provide victims of unlawful discrim-
ination with a remedy. His pardon suggested President
Trump's willingness to compromise constitutional norms
to reward an ally.

That said, the pardon of Arpaio is not by itself impeachable. The framers intended the pardon power to be

broad, and while the pardon of Arpaio may be regrettable, the idea of generosity toward an octogenarian with a long career in law enforcement, the stated rationale for the pardon, cannot be said to be beyond the constitutional pale. Indeed, the last several presidents all delivered pardons as controversial and dubious as the pardon of Arpaio.

Much of the above also applies to Trump's pardon of Scooter Libby, a former high-ranking White House official convicted in 2007 of several charges based on lying to a special prosecutor investigating the leaking of the covert identity of a CIA agent. The official statement accompanying the pardon cited "credible evidence" of Libby's innocence and his "more than a decade of honorable service to the nation."[18] While, as noted, the latter is not a traditional basis for a pardon, both of these justifications fall within the president's broad prerogatives.

Concern stems from suspicion that the real motive for the Libby pardon was to signal several former Trump aides, either indicted or under investigation, that if they held steady and declined to offer prosecutors evidence of the president's wrongdoing, they would be rewarded with pardons of their own. If that were indeed the principal motive, it would amount to using a presidential power for the purpose of impeding law enforcement—surely justifying impeachment. It would, however, be exceptionally difficult to prove that this was the president's motive, and Congress should not impeach based on suspicion.

Media reports indicate that President Trump has inquired about the viability of pardoning *himself*. Knowing that a self-pardon is a possibility down the road, the issue warrants discussion.

Questions about the propriety of a self-pardon have kicked around since the final days of the Nixon presidency in 1974, when his Office of Legal Counsel issued an opinion that he lacked that authority. Several pardon attorneys and other experts, including Solicitor General Robert Bork, disagreed. The issue arose again at the end of George H.W. Bush's term in 1992, when Bush's pardon of government officials involved in the Iran-Contra affair prompted speculation that he might pardon himself. Experts were again divided on whether a president has that authority. Ditto when the question emerged during Bill Clinton's travails.

When word got out in July 2017 that President Trump had asked his lawyers about the self-pardon, legal experts again produced a split decision. Interestingly, some on both sides regarded the question as a no-brainer. Alan Dershowitz criticized both sides: "Can the president pardon himself? The answer is crystal clear! And anyone who gives you a different answer is misleading you, because there is only one correct answer. Here it is: Nobody knows!"[19]

Dershowitz has a point. The founding fathers did not address the self-pardon question, no president has attempted to pardon himself, and no court has addressed the question. How is it, then, that experts on both sides seem cocksure? The answer is that each side has at its disposal a powerful argument that, seen a certain way, looks self-evident.

Those who say that President Trump can pardon himself cite the Constitution's unambiguous language. As noted, Article II places no limits on whom the president may pardon. While unclear textual provisions demand interpretation, clear ones demand obedience. Moreover, if the framers started placing limits on the pardon power, where would they stop? If it is absurd for someone to pardon himself, isn't it also problematic to pardon one's family? How about close friends and associates? To start down this slippery slope would create difficult distinctions and erode the president's authority as the last safeguard against criminal punishment.

But the opposite argument is also strong, rooted in the age-old principle that no person shall be a judge in his or her own case. Blackstone, the great British legal historian, considered this a sacred principle, and our founding fathers cited it routinely, including James Madison in *The Federalist*. Moreover, the U.S. Constitution directly played a variation on this theme. The vice president presides over the Senate with one single exception: during an impeachment trial of the president. (In that instance, the chief justice presides.) The framers recognized a disqualifying conflict of interest preventing the person next in line from presiding over the president's trial, but the conflict is obviously even greater if the president pardons himself.

Note that the Constitution does not state that the vice president cannot preside at his *own* impeachment trial. That literally went without saying. It may be that the same is true when it comes to the idea of the president pardoning him- or herself.

For present purposes, it does not matter which of the competing views on presidential self-pardon is correct. Let us suppose for the sake of argument that the president does indeed have absolute pardon power, including the power to self-pardon: Any court must honor the self-pardon and forbid criminal prosecution. It does not follow, however, that the president cannot be impeached for this action. (He could not pardon himself with respect to the impeachment, for the Constitution explicitly says that the pardon power does not extend to impeachments.) To the contrary, improper use of the pardon power, like improper use of any executive branch power, could justify impeachment.

Absent a most unusual situation, a presidential self-pardon would violate rather than advance the legitimate purposes of the pardon power. As a sitting president probably cannot be indicted, any self-pardon would be prospective—granted before the president was charged, much less convicted. Thus, the president would not be self-pardoning because of wrongful conviction or an overly harsh punishment.

The pre-prosecution pardon is unusual and requires special justification, such as Gerald Ford's belief that the prosecution of Richard Nixon would have hampered Ford's own presidency. And Ford's pardon of Nixon, far from supporting the idea of a self-pardon, shows why it is unnecessary. If a president perceives that his prosecution will harm the nation, there is a ready remedy: pardon by the *next* president, whose judgment would be less clouded by self-interest. To the extent Ford's motives were questioned, with suspicions that he agreed to pardon Nixon in exchange for the latter resigning, it only reinforces the problems of self-pardon, which involve an even more blatant conflict of interest.

So too, there is reason to doubt that the president's self-pardon will enhance national tranquility. Again, the next president would be the better judge of that, and more generally, the better judge of whether the pardon would serve the public interest. The self-pardon may well be motivated by something other than justice, mercy, or the public interest. More likely it will reflect self-favoritism. Few would dispute that a president who uses the pardon power solely to reward family, friends, or campaign contributors misuses it. How much more so if used for self-pardon.

That such action will typically be impeachable starts with the fact that the president who self-pardons effectively admits to guilt in underlying crimes. (The Supreme Court has said that acceptance of a pardon amounts to admission of guilt. In the case of a self-pardon, administering and accepting are inseparable.) By definition, such a president would also transgress the time-honored principle that no person can judge his or her own case.

We need to recall that the Constitution sharply separates the processes for impeachment and criminal law. The former can happen only to a sitting president and cannot result in punishment beyond loss of office; the latter can happen only to one no longer in office, and can result in incarceration. As a matter of criminal law, perhaps the president can self-pardon and thereby immunize himself from criminal punishment once she leaves office. But such action can hasten the day she leaves office because it constitutes potentially impeachable behavior. If the current president or any other should remove himself from legal jeopardy, Congress should consider removing him from political office as well.

RECEIPT OF EMOLUMENTS

Article I, Section 9, Clause 8 of the Constitution declares that no U.S. officeholder may, without consent of Congress, "accept [ ] any present, Emolument, Office or Title, of any kind whatever, from any King, Prince, or foreign State."

Since emoluments are generally defined as any fee or profit, and President Trump's hotels, golf courses, and restaurants are visited by foreign leaders, the violation of the Emoluments Clause might seem to go without saying. Not surprisingly, several lawsuits (one by state attorneys general, one by members of Congress, and one by a citizen watchdog group) have been filed alleging such a violation.

The foreign Emoluments Clause, categorically worded (barring a gift or emolument "*of any kind whatever*"), stemmed from concern about foreigners essentially bribing U.S. officials in order to attain or increase influence. Note that the Clause bans emoluments regardless of whether there is a quid pro quo. The drafters wished for officeholders to avoid any temptation to impropriety. And while President Trump has allegedly transferred day-to-day control of his businesses to his children, he continues to visit some of these businesses—country clubs, golf courses, hotels, restaurants—and remains their ultimate beneficiary, so the potential conflicts of interest are undiminished.

In briefs defending against the lawsuits, Trump's lawyers argue that the Emoluments Clause precludes only benefits given to the president in his official capacity or from services he personally provides, and that "fair market exchanges" involving his businesses are exempt. But these arguments seem at odds with the language and purpose of the clause.

Law dictionaries define emoluments as "monies that have been received for services given or for reimbursements"—exactly what happens when, for example, people pay for their room at the Trump Hotel. Dr. Samuel Johnson's dictionary, published two years before America's Constitutional Convention in 1787, defined "emolument" broadly as a "profit or advantage." No founding-era dictionary supports a narrower definition that would exempt the patronage of Trump's businesses. Lest there by any doubt that they intended a broad reading of the prohibition, the framers included "presents" as well as "emoluments" and, as noted, added "of any kind whatever."

The ban on emoluments guards against foreign

influence. Joseph Story, the great 19th-century Supreme Court justice and legal historian, explained that the framers so dreaded foreign influence that they "put [ ] it out of the power of any officer of government" to decide what benefits to accept from foreign countries.[20] President Trump stands to benefit personally from the patronage of his various businesses, presenting the real risk that foreign countries will attempt to curry favor with him through such patronage or by granting his businesses favorable treatment within their borders.

The case of President Trump's relationship with Rodrigo Duterte, the ruthless president of the Philippines, illustrates the concerns underlying the Foreign Emoluments Clause. Duterte has reportedly ordered his police (and others) to kill thousands of people suspected of involvement in the drug trade. Trump has publicly praised Duterte. It may be that Trump sees Duterte as an ally in the war on drugs, but skeptics cite Trump's extensive business involvements with the Philippines, including his $150 million Trump Tower in Manila.

There has also been speculation that his business interests in China have affected his decision-making. Trump had spent a fortune over the course of a decade seeking a trademark for the use of his name in construction projects in China. Shortly after he took office, the Chinese government granted him preliminary approval, made final two days after Trump confirmed that he would not pursue the "two-China" policy that the Chinese vehemently oppose. China has since approved dozens of Trump trademarks, and he has not kept his campaign promise to seek punishment of China as a currency manipulator.

Coincidence? Quid pro quo? Thanks to the Emoluments Clause, we should not be put in the position of trying to determine that. The Philippines and China present only two examples of how President Trump's business interests could affect how he treats foreign nations and vice versa. His business interests extend around the globe. It does not follow that someone in Trump's position cannot serve as president. He could seek congressional approval (which the Emoluments Clause explicitly authorizes) or divest his holdings.

We have been focusing on foreign emoluments, but there is also a potential problem resulting from Trump's extensive business activities within the United States. Article II, Section 1, Clause 7, the so-called "Domestic Emoluments Clause," refers to the president's salary and says he "shall not receive [during his term in office] any other emolument from the United States or any of them." Trump's businesses have received numerous benefits from states, such as discretionary tax credits, in possible violation of the prohibition on domestic emoluments. (These, too, are alleged in the various lawsuits against him.)

In *Federalist* 73, Alexander Hamilton discussed the Domestic Emoluments Clause. Hamilton considered it self-evident that the president should receive no benefits other than his salary, including no emoluments. Rather, the president's sole interest should be the good of the country, uncompromised by conflicts created by possible private gain: "He can, of course, have no pecuniary inducement to renounce or desert the independence intended for him by the Constitution."

President Trump's domestic business interests arguably violate this principle. All 50 states are motivated to take actions, directly or indirectly, that affect Trump's financial holdings. Indeed, even if they wanted to, states could not avoid taking actions that affect his interests, since routine fiscal and regulatory measures necessarily have such an effect.

If Trump is in violation of the foreign or domestic emoluments clauses, a strong case can be made that he has committed an impeachable offense. After all, these clauses are part of the Constitution itself.

And yet, Trump's receipt of emoluments does not warrant impeachment at this time. Case law on the emoluments clauses barely exists and Trump is entitled to a court finding of his alleged violations. Some Trump supporters have floated the argument that the Foreign Emoluments Clause does not apply to presidents. While this and other defenses against Trump's apparent violations may seem strained, they could yet prevail. Or courts may find that no one has standing to bring such claims, in which case Congress should address the matter. (Two courts have weighed in on this issue, reaching opposite conclusions about standing.)

Impeachment on the basis of unconstitutional receipt of emoluments should be considered only if President

Trump fails to comply with a relevant court order or a determination by some other qualified body such as Congress or his own Office of Legal Counsel.

PAYOFFS TO STORMY DANIELS AND KAREN MCDOUGAL

The criminal conviction of Trump's personal attorney and "fixer," Michael Cohen, yielded another possible basis of impeachment. On August 21, 2018, Cohen pled guilty in federal court to eight charges, two of them stemming from payments to porn star Stormy Daniels and former Playboy model Karen McDougal ($130,000 and $150,000, respectively) in exchange for their silence about alleged trysts with Trump. Because the payments were made during the latter stages of the 2016 presidential campaign and were motivated by a desire to assist Trump's candidacy, they constituted a violation of campaign finance laws—an in-kind contribution to the Trump campaign that wasn't reported and that vastly exceeded the maximum contribution of $2,700.

For present purposes, the crucial question concerns Trump's participation in these violations. He has denied the relationships, and knowledge of the payments in advance, but in open court Cohen declared that he made the payments at Trump's behest. If Cohen is telling the truth, would Trump's behavior be impeachable?

The answer is no, with respect to the alleged affairs themselves. A president's adulterous relationship before he became president is less malignant than actions by Bill Clinton that should not have given rise to impeachment. (Clinton's affair with Monica Lewinsky occurred while he was in office and gave rise to perjury.) Trump's possible complicity in the violation of campaign finance laws is more significant. It may seem that such actions, though potentially criminal, are too minor to amount to impeachable offenses. As we have noted, statutory crimes do not automatically qualify as *constitutional* high crimes and misdemeanors.

However, the alleged conduct here involves more than a technical violation of campaign finance laws of the sort routinely committed, often inadvertently, by political campaigns. Here, the payments of hush money were apparently designed to prevent the dissemination of information that could have affected the outcome of the election. If the president was involved in such conduct, impeachment could be justified.

CONCLUDING THOUGHTS

Of the various charges leveled against President Trump, conspiracy with Russia and obstruction of justice are the ones that, if such behavior occurred, most clearly merit impeachment. At least based on the evidence developed thus far, his other allegedly improper actions probably do not independently justify Trump's impeachment. However, it does not follow that the non-impeachable actions are irrelevant if and when Congress contemplates impeachment.

We must keep in mind the "rotten store" metaphor discussed in connection with Richard Nixon, the idea that a pattern of improper actions forfeits the president's presumption against impeachment. In this connection, we must observe the wide range of conduct by president Trump, including not only actions discussed above but also seeking to prevent Muslims from entering the country; pressuring his attorney general to resign because the latter recused himself rather than do the president's bidding with respect to the special counsel's investigation; recklessly accusing former President Obama of ordering wiretapping of Trump Tower; attacking the Justice department, FBI, and individual federal judges; downplaying the actions of white supremacists; and waging an assault on the media (including calling them "the enemy of the people" and threatening to restrict their freedom) that arguably contradicts the spirit of the First Amendment.[21]

People may disagree about the extent of impropriety of some of these actions, but the overarching point should be uncontroversial: If members of Congress are uncertain whether any of the president's specific offenses warrant his removal, they may consider whether the administration has systematically compromised constitutional and democratic norms and the dignity of the office.

CONCLUSION

Some commentators about impeachment offer an over-arching theory or definition of what constitutes high crimes and misdemeanors. I have not attempted that here because I do not believe it is possible. For example, almost everyone agrees that a president who commits murder must be removed from office even if the act occurred in a private setting unrelated to his official responsibilities. Virtually everyone would also agree that a private offense of little consequence, such as a traffic violation, could not possibly be impeachable. But where does one draw the line separating the two sets of cases? Armed robbery? Simple assault? Passing a bad check?

Every potential impeachment case must be considered in all its particulars. Still, we are fortunate to have guidance both from the founders and from three presidential impeachment episodes spread across 130 years. While these cases do not yield a tidy theory of what constitutes an impeachable offense, they do help us derive generally valid lessons for approaching each case. These lessons prove useful whenever removing the president is contemplated, and in the previous chapter I have tried to apply those lessons to the various prospective charges against President Trump.

I shall close by pulling back from the present situation and seeking to regain a glimpse of the big picture.

The Declaration of Independence did more than assert the birth of a nation. It justified breaking away from Great Britain, and made a permanent statement of profound importance. We tend to focus on the first sentence of the second paragraph: "We hold these truths to be self-evident, that all men are created equal, that they are endowed by their creator with certain unalienable rights, that among these are life, liberty and the pursuit of happiness." But the next two sentences are equally key: "That to secure these rights, governments are instituted among men, deriving their just powers from the consent of the governed — That whenever any form of government becomes destructive of these ends, it is the right of the people to alter or to abolish it, and to institute new government."

In other words, in order to protect individual rights to life, liberty, and the pursuit of happiness, the People also retain an inalienable right to act collectively to "alter or to abolish" and recompose our government. Note that altering and abolishing are not the same thing, and that the ability to alter our government avoids the need for revolution (or *abolishing* our government). We can think of impeachment as a means of alteration—a change at the top without the normal process of election.

Thomas Jefferson and his fellow founders did not intend their sentiment about altering and abolishing government as rhetorical fluff. Rather, they justified the colonial rebellion by virtue of "popular sovereignty"—the People own the government. This idea finds further expression in the opening line of the Constitution: "We the People of the United States . . . do ordain and establish this Constitution for the United States of America."

The Declaration of Independence and the Preamble to the Constitution worked in tandem. The People announced and exercised their rights to break free of an oppressor and to establish their own government. Both documents imply that We the People today—women and men of all stripes—collectively retain the sovereign right to do so again if circumstances require.

The Declaration of Independence set forth the many abuses we suffered at the hands of the British Crown. In the future, it could be a different set of circumstances that would compel the People to alter or abolish their own government. We may do so, in the words of the Declaration, "whenever any form of government becomes destructive of these ends"—that is, whenever the government denies our inalienable rights or forfeits its legitimacy. Alexander Hamilton expressed this collective right even more broadly in *Federalist* 78, citing "that fundamental principle of republican government which admits the right of the people to alter or abolish the established Constitution *whenever they find it inconsistent with their happiness*."[1]

Any sentiment that united Thomas Jefferson and Alexander Hamilton, adversaries with fundamentally different visions, should make us sit up and take notice. But it is not surprising that Jefferson and Hamilton agreed on what was literally the first principle of the United States of America: The People employ the government, and therefore may change the government.

In making this point repeatedly (in the Declaration, the Constitution, and *The Federalist*), the founders were not advocating frequent resort to revolution. Again, they championed the right to *alter* or abolish the government, and alterations involve less than regime change. The Constitution explicitly provides means for alteration, especially Article V's provision for amendment. The availability of such peaceful means of changing our governing charter ensured that we would turn to full-scale revolution only as a very last resort. As noted, impeachment offers another path for alteration.

At the conclusion of the Constitutional Convention in Philadelphia in 1787, someone asked Benjamin Franklin what form of government the delegates had produced, and Franklin is said to have replied, "A Republic, Sir, if you can keep it."[2] Maintaining our democratic republic requires alterations from time to time. It also requires vigilance. The Constitution placed impediments in the way of would-be tyrants, but keeping our republic is a permanent project. The founders gave us a workable form of self-government, and the tools to preserve it, but unless we use those tools well and wisely, it will all be for naught.

Impeachment is a crucial tool when it comes to protecting our democracy. Let us use it well and wisely.

ENDNOTES

Introduction

1 Sari Horowitz and Philip Rucker, "A Bold New Defense: Presidents Cannot Obstruct Justice," *Washington Post*, December 4, 2017.

2 Max Farrand, ed., *Records of the Constitutional Convention of 1787* (New Haven, CT: Yale University Press, 1911), vol. 2, p. 65.

3 Jonathan Elliot, *The Debates in the Several State Conventions on the Adoption of the Federal Constitution* (Ithaca, NY: Cornell University, 2009), vol. 1, p. 467.

Chapter One

1 Merrill Peterson, ed., *The Portable Thomas Jefferson* (New York: Penguin, 1975) (letter to George Hay, June 20, 1807), p. 156.

2 119 *Congressional Record* 11913 (April 15, 1970).

3 Farrand, *Records of the Constitutional Convention*, vol. 2, p. 550.

4 Ibid.

5 Clinton Rossiter, ed., *The Federalist Papers*, (New York: New American Library, 1961), p. 396.

Chapter Two

1 Chester Hearn, *The Impeachment of Andrew Johnson* (North Carolina: McFarland, 2007), p. 41.

2 W.E. Burghardt Du Bois, *Black Reconstruction in America 1860-80* (New York: Free Press, 1998), p. 259.

3 William Teignmouth Shore, *Charles Dickens and his Friends* (Ithaca, NY: Cornell University Library, 1909), p. 296.

4 John Y. Simon, *The Papers of Ulysses S Grant: January 1–September 30, 1867* (Carbondale: Southern Illinois University Press, 1991), vol. 17, p. 269.

5 David Miller Dewitt, *The Impeachment and Trial of Andrew Johnson* (New York: Macmillan, 1903), p. 175.

6 Ibid., 396.

7 Theodore Clarke Smith, *The Life and Letters of James Abram Garfield: 1831-77* (Hamden, CT: Archon Books, 1868), p. 424.

8 Dewitt, *The Impeachment and Trial of Andrew Johnson*, p. 401.

9 Ibid., 402.

10 John Labovitz, *Presidential Impeachment* (New Haven, CT: Yale University Press, 1978), p. 66.

11 Dewitt, *The Impeachment and Trial of Andrew Johnson*, p. 415.

12 Ibid., 416.

13 Benjamin Perley Poore, *The Trial of Andrew Johnson, President of the United States, Before the Senate of the United States in Impeachment by the House of Representatives for High Crimes and Misdemeanors* (Andesite Press, 2015), p. 629.

14 Ibid., 82.

15 Ibid.

16 Labovitz, *Presidential Impeachment*, p. 72.

17 Poore, *The Trial of Andrew Johnson*, p. 266.

18 Ibid., 307.

19 Ibid., 273.

20 Ibid.

21 Ibid., 301.

22 Ibid., 325.

23 Ibid., 468.

24 Dewitt, *The Impeachment and Trial of Andrew Johnson*, p. 413.

25 Richard Ruddy, *Edmund G. Ross, Soldier, Senator, Abolitionist* (Albuquerque: University of New Mexico Press, 2013), p. 136.

26 Warren Bowen, *Andrew Johnson and the Negro* (Knoxville: University of Tennessee Press, 1989), p. 142.

27 Poore, *The Trial of Andrew Johnson*, p. 247.

28 Dewitt, *The Impeachment and Trial of Andrew Johnson*, p. 584.

29 Poore, *The Trial of Andrew Johnson*, p. 328.

Chapter Three

1 *Public Papers of the Presidents of the United States, Richard Nixon* (Washington: Government Printing Office, 1967), p. 952.

2 Stanley Kutler, ed., *Watergate: A Brief History with Documents* (Malden, MA: Wiley-Blackwell, 2010), p. 30.

3 Theodore White, *Breach of Faith: the Fall of Richard Nixon* (New York: Dell, 1986), p. 243.

4 Elizabeth Drew, *Washington Journal: The Events of 1973–1974* (New York: Random House, 1974), p. 69.

5 Carroll Kilpatrick, "Nixon Tells Editors, 'I'm not a crook'" *Washington Post*, November 18, 1973, p. A1.

6 Sam Ervin, *The Whole Truth: The Watergate Conspiracy* (New York: Random House, 1980), p. 26.

7 *Impeachment: Selected Materials* (Washington: U.S. Government Printing Office, 1998), p. 27.

8 Drew, *Washington Journal*, p. 227.

9 *Public Papers of the Presidents of the United States, Richard Nixon*, 391.

10 Clifton Daniel, "Leaks: A Fact of Life," *New York Times*, June 29, 1974.

11 Ervin, *The Whole Truth*, p. 272.

12 Drew, *Washington Journal*, p. 322.

13 Ibid., 323.

14 Stephen Stathis, *Landmark Speeches in Congress: From the Declaration of Independence to the War in Iraq* (Washington: CQ Press, 2009), p. 423.

15 Annie Groer, "Larry Hogan, Chip Off the Ol' Block," *Roll Call*, June 22, 2016.

16 Drew, *Washington Journal*, p. 346.

17 Ibid., 348.

18 Ibid., 398.

Chapter Four

1 *Referral from Independent Counsel Kenneth Starr in Conformity with the Requirements of Title 28 United States Code Section 585(c)* (Washington: U.S. Government Printing Office, 1998).

2 "Conyers Opening Remarks on Inquiry," *Washington Post*, October 5, 1998.

3 Edwin Chen, "Watergate Words Ring During Debate," *Los Angeles Times*, October 6, 1998.

4 David P. Schippers, *Sellout: The Inside Story of President Clinton's Impeachment* (Washington: Regnery, 2000), p.75.

5 Peter Baker, *The Breach: Inside the Impeachment and Trial of*

William Jefferson Clinton (New York: Scribner, 2000), p. 122.

6 "The Impeachment Hearings: Ranking Member Rep. John Conyers' Opening Statement," *Washington Post*, November 19, 1998.

7 Ibid.

8 Baker, *The Breach*, p. 174.

9 Ibid., 180.

10 Ibid., 184.

11 Ibid.

12 Ibid., 203.

13 Ibid., 205.

14 Ibid., p. 206.

15 John Broder, "Contrite Clinton Invites Censure," *New York Times*, December 12, 1998.

16 "Full Text of Livingston Statement," *CNN.com*, December 17, 1998.

17 "Henry Hyde Opening Statement," *Washington Post*, December 18, 1998.

18 "Richard Gephart Opening Statement," *Washington Post*, December 18, 1998.

19 Ruth Marcus, "Respect Election or 'Cleanse the Office'?" *Washington Post*, January 17, 1999.

20 "Transcript: former Senator Dale Bumpers," *CNN.com*, January 21, 1999.

21 Baker, *The Breach*, p. 334.

22 Ibid., 342.

23 Ibid.

24 Ibid., 394.

Chapter Five

1 Farrand, *Records of the Constitutional Convention of 1787*, vol. 2, p. 427.

2 Jody Baumgartner, *The American Vice Presidency Reconsidered* (Westport: Praeger, 2006), p. 3.

3 Michael Beschloss, "The Vice President Who Pulled a Gun on Truman," *New York Times*, April 22, 2014.

4 David McCullough, *John Adams* (New York: Simon & Schuster, 2002), p. 402.

5 John Feerick, *The Twenty-fifth Amendment: Its Complete History and Applications* (New York: Fordham University Press, 1992), p. 10.

6 Richard Nixon, *Six Crises* (New York: Doubleday, 1962), p. 144.

7 James Reston, "Why America Weeps: Kennedy Victim of Violent Streak He Sought to Curb in the Nation," *New York Times*, November 23, 1963.

8 *Public Papers of the Presidents of the United States, Lyndon B. Johnson* (Washington: Government Printing Office, 1967), vol. 2, p. 8.

9 Feerick, *The Twenty-fifth Amendment*, p. 214.

10 Ross Douthat, "The Twenty-fifth Amendment Solution for Removing Trump," *New York Times*, May 16, 2017.

Chapter Six

1 Jonathan Chait, "Scandal TBD," *New Republic*, October 6, 2010.

2 William Rehnquist, *Grand Inquests: The Historic Impeachments of Samuel Chase and President Andrew Johnson* (New York: William Morrow, 1992), p. 125.

3 Charles Black, *Impeachment: A Handbook* (New Haven, CT: Yale University Press, 1974), p. 12.

4 Farrand, *Records of the Constitutional Convention of 1787*, vol. 1, p. 86.

5 *Trial of Andrew Johnson, President of the United States, Before the Senate of the United States on Impeachment of the House of Representatives for High Crimes and Misdemeanors* (Washington: Government Printing Office, 1868), vol. 3, p. 248.

6 H. Lowell Brown, *High Crimes and Misdemeanors in Presidential Impeachment* (New York: Palgrave and MacMillan, 2010), p. 56.

7 Christopher Lydon, "Richardson Sidesteps Constitutional Issues," *New York Times*, October 24, 1973.

8 Black, *Impeachment: A Handbook*, p. 3.

9 Richard Posner, *An Affair of State* (Cambridge, MA: Harvard University Press, 1999), p. 91. (Emphasis in original.)

10 Drew, *Washington Journal*, p. 329.

11 Ibid., 219.

Chapter Seven

1 See Jo Becker, Adam Goldman, and Matt Apizzo, "Russia Dirt on Clinton? 'I Love it' Donald Trump Jr. said," *New York Times*, July 11, 2017.

2 Ashley Parker and David E. Sanger, "Donald Trump Calls on Russia to Find Hillary Clinton's Missing E-mails," *New York Times*, July 27, 2016.

3 See Abby Phillip, "O'Reilly told Trump that Putin is a killer. Trump's reply: 'You think our country is so innocent?'" *Washington Post*, February 4, 2017.

4 See Matthew Cooper, "Will Trump's Smear of McCain Doom His Candidacy?" *Newsweek*, July 18, 2015.

5 Farrand, *Records of the Constitutional Convention*, vol. 2, p. 66.

6 Ibid., 68.

7 Black, *Impeachment: A Handbook*, p. 46. (Emphasis in original.)

8 Ibid.

9 Ibid. (Emphasis in original.)

10 See Barbara Radnofsky, *A Citizen's Guide to Impeachment* (Brooklyn, NY: Melville House, 2017), p. 16.

11 *The Federalist Papers*, 447.

12 Ibid., 448.

13 Ibid., 449.

14 Washington's Seventh Annual Address to Congress, in James D. Richardson, *A Compilation of the Messages and Papers of the President, 1789–1897* (Washington: Government Printing Office, 1896), vol. 1, p. 184.

15 *Biddle v. Perovich*, 274 U.S. 480 (1927).

16 *The Federalist Papers*, p. 448.

17 See Devlin Barrett and Abby Phillip, "Trump Pardons Former Arizona Sheriff Joe Arpaio," *Washington Post*, August 25, 2017.

18 See S.A. Miller and Dave Boyer, "Trump's Pardon of Libby

in 2007 Conviction Reverberates Through Washington," *Washington Times*, April 15, 2018.

19 Alan Dershowitz, "Can the President Pardon Himself?" *The Hill*, July 26, 2017.

20 Joseph Story, *Commentaries on the Constitution*, vol. 3, Section 1346 (1833).

21 Michael Grynbaum, "Trump Calls the News Media 'The Enemy of the American People,'" *New York Times*, February 17, 2017.

Conclusion

1 *The Federalist Papers*, 469.

2 This oft-quoted Franklin line, the stuff of lore, has not been traced to its original source.

ACKNOWLEDGMENTS

First, special thanks to Greg Ruggiero and John Richard for their belief in this project and their help bringing it to fruition.

To Sheldon Hirsch, for reading and providing thoughtful comments on parts, and Sarah Hirsch, Joni Hirsch, David Halperin, Howard Shapiro, and Chris Merkling, for reading and commenting on entire drafts. Evan Caminker, David Shipler, and Alan Morrison, as is their wont, went above and beyond, reading and commenting on multiple drafts. Marjorie Hirsch was, as always, my first and last reader, and I am more grateful than she can know. Their numerous suggestions, large and small, have enriched this project.

ABOUT THE AUTHOR

Alan Hirsch, Instructor in the Humanities and Chair of the Justice and Law Studies program at Williams College, is the author of numerous works of legal scholarship and many books, including *For the People: What the Constitution Really Says About Your Rights* (coauthored with Akhil Amar) and *A Citizen's Guide to Impeachment*. He received a J.D. from Yale Law School and B.A. from Amherst College. His work has appeared in the *Washington Post*, *Los Angeles Times*, *Washington Times*, *Newsday*, and the *Village Voice*. Hirsch also serves as a trial consultant and expert witness on interrogations and false confessions, testifying around the nation. He lives in Williamstown, Massachusetts, with his wife, Marjorie.